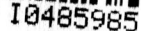

The 3-By-5 Steps:

to Pass Your PMP® Certification

BONUS: 200 Practice Questions

FJ. RUSSO

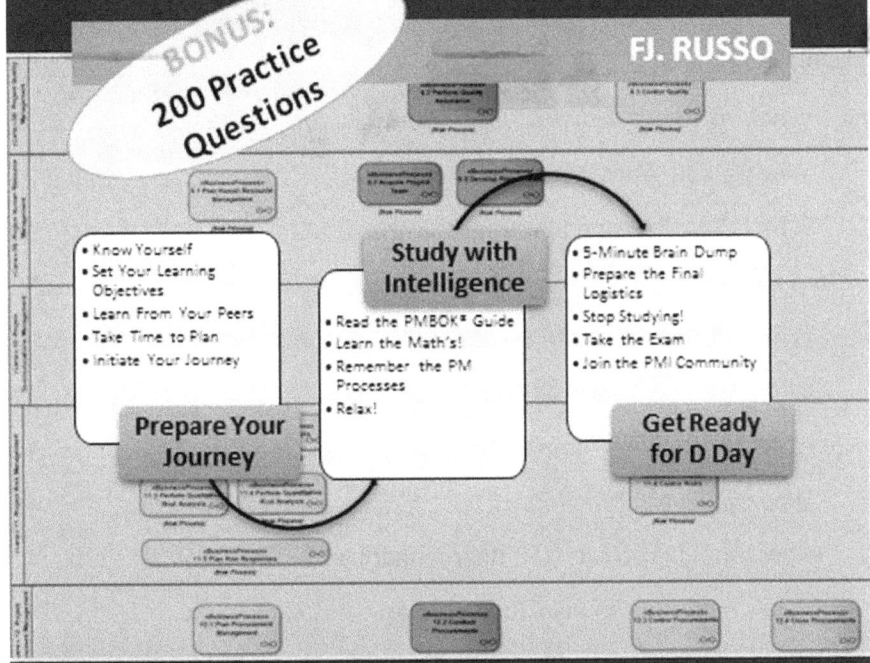

- Know Yourself
- Set Your Learning Objectives
- Learn From Your Peers
- Take Time to Plan
- Initiate Your Journey

Prepare Your Journey

Study with Intelligence

- Read the PMBOK® Guide
- Learn the Math's!
- Remember the PM Processes
- Relax!

- 5-Minute Brain Dump
- Prepare the Final Logistics
- Stop Studying!
- Take the Exam
- Join the PMI Community

Get Ready for D Day

Table of Contents

Disclaimer

The data and information provided in this document and any references to services are provided on an "*as is*" basis for information purposes only without any warranties or representations of any kind whatsoever, whether express or implied, all of which are hereby disclaimed, including without limitation any warranties of merchantability, fitness for a particular purpose, title and non-infringement.

In no event shall FJ. RUSSO and/or its suppliers be liable for any special, indirect, or consequential damages or any damages whatsoever resulting from loss of use, data or profits, whether in an action of contract, negligence, or other tortious action, arising out of or in connection with the use of the information in, or obtained through, this document.

Registered Marks

All brand, product, service, and process names appearing is in this document are trademarks of their respective holders. Reference to or use of a product, service, or process does not imply recommendation, approval, affiliation, or sponsorship of that product, service, or process by FJ. RUSSO. Nothing contained herein shall be construed as conferring by any means any license or right under any patent, copyright, trademark, or other intellectual property right of the Company or any third party, except as expressly granted herein.

PMI, the PMI Logo, PMP, PMBOK, PgMP, *"Project Management Journal"*, *"PM Network"*, and the PMI Today logo are registered marks of Project Management Institute, Inc.

Preface

PMP® stands for **Project Management Professional**. The PMP Certification is a credential offered by the Project Management Institute (PMI). To be certified, you must pass an exam called the PMP exam.

What is the PMP exam?

The PMP exam is based on the Project Management Body of Knowledge (PMBOK) ® Guide, which describes tasks out of five domains: Initiating, Planning, Executing, Monitoring and Controlling, and Closing the project.

The exam consists of 200 multiple choice questions. 25 of the 200 questions are *"sample"* questions and are not counted for or against the test taker. The test taker is scored on their proficiency on the remaining 175 questions.

Why passing the PMP exam?

Since you have already embarked onto your Project Management Certification journey, you must be aware of the industry drivers to take and pass the PMP Exam.

Based on our friends on Wikipedia, government, commercial and other organizations primarily employ PMP Certified Project Managers in an attempt to improve the success rate of projects in all areas of knowledge, by applying a standardized and evolving set of project management principles as contained in the *PMBOK® Guide*.

In December 2005, the PMP credential was tied for fourth place in CertCities.com's 10 hottest certifications for 2006, and in December 2008, it was number 7 of ZDNet's 10 best IT certifications. More recently, in 2012 and 2013, the PMP credential has been ranked as a **top certification by CIO**, Global Knowledge, and About.com.

In 2014, the **PMP Certification was rated #1 most valuable** by IT Career Finder in their "*Top 10 Highest Paying IT Certifications for 2014.*" Outside of IT, the PMP ranked #5 with Global Knowledge "*15 Top-Paying*

Certifications for 2014," and #8 with Careerealism "Top 10 Professional Certifications for a Bright Future."

Thus, if you would like to boost your project management career, the PMP Certification is definitively a qualification you need to add to your toolset.

Who can take the PMP Exam?

As many other professional certifications, to take the PMP exam, you must meet a certain numbers of pre-requisites:

- You must have completed a high school diploma or an Associate degree with 60 months (7,500 hours) of project management experience, or
- Your must have a Bachelor's degree with 36 months (4,500 hours) of project management experience

In both cases, candidates must also have 35 hours of project management education.

Now, in the event you do not meet the requisite experience to take the PMP Exam, I greatly encourage you to consider the Certified Associate in Project Management (CAPM) ®, another certification offered by the Project Management Institute. Most steps and project management concepts discussed in this book are applicable to the CAPM exam as well.

Fast Forward

Since time goes by so quickly, when I read a book, and especially a book focusing on an area I am interested in, I just want the author to get to the point... faster!

Hence, below are the key 3-By-5 Steps sections you should read and follow to pass your PMP Certification.

Use the links and page indicators to easily navigate:

The 3-By-5 Steps		Links
9	Simulate the Exam	Step #9: Simulate the Exam (104)
10	Don't Forget to Relax	
11	Train for a 5-Minute Brain Dump	Exercise: I write-down all the formulas... (113) Exercise: I write-down all the processes... (115)
12	Prepare the Final Logistics	Step #12: Prepare the Final Logistics (117)
13	Stop Studying and Sleep Well	
14	Start your Exam with Confidence	Step #14: Start your Exam with Confidence (123)
15	Join the PMI Community	Step #15: Join the PMI Community (124)
	BONUS	Bonus: 200-Question Practice Exam. (129)

Introduction

A few years back (not to say four decades ago), when I was still a kid, as soon as the school year was over, with anticipation, my brother and I would look forward to our family vacation.

Every year, late July, my parents were taking a couple of weeks off from their busy life to travel around our mesmerizing home country: Italy.

Since we lived near Santa Marinella, near the most marvelous beaches of Italy (as far as I remember), we were always heading in the opposite direction of the Mediterranean Sea and its many tourists. And so, every year, my parents were packing our old Fiat with all the necessary gears, and just like that, we were on our way to Aosta, Bergamo, Florence, Turin, or Sondrio. Sometimes we were even crossing the borders, driving North, East or West, to Switzerland, Liechtenstein, France, or Austria.

From these road trips and vacations, I only keep incredibly memories; my parents were happy, forgetting the stress of their daily work. My brother and I were not fighting over anything kids care about. We were a family, enjoying every moments, hiking, resting, eating outdoors, running, swimming in anonymous lakes, and biking.

To be honest, my older brother and I did not have much to say about where we will be heading for our family vacation: my parents were the ones deciding, and the children (my brother and I) were following. I have to admit that, at the time, I did not like my complete lack of choice.

Now, however, as a parent, and as a project manager, I totally understand the reasons why my brother and I did not have anything to say about our destination.

We were not the project sponsors; my parents were.

My brother and I, we were stakeholders – important stakeholders with a certain degree of influence but, we still had to do what our parents asked.

To put this more clearly:

Everything we do in life has
a) **A scope,**
b) **A cost, and**
c) **A defined timeline.**

Everything we do – even going on a family vacation – can be considered as a project with clear and well-defined boundaries that we must understand and respect.

If as a child, I would have had the opportunity to weigh in into the decision on where we were going to go, I would have disregarded two critical components of the decision-making process: the timeline and the cost; I would have indeed asked my parents to spend months traveling, discarding completely how expensive it would have been.

To make a long story short, I did not have a clue.

And so, my parents were the ones scoping our yearly vacation and deciding. Does it make sense?

On the other hand, my parents also knew how essential it was for my older brother and me to feel involved into the decision making process and, contribute to the preparatory activities of our vacation.

Thus, a couple of weeks before our scheduled departure, my parents would organize a family meeting. After dining, instead of playing cards, scrabble, a board game, listening to the radio, or watching television, my parents would unveil their plan. Looking forward to our upcoming vacation, my brother and I were interestingly focused and all ears.

A couple of years (especially when we went to Florence) it was clear that we were not so excited about my parents' plan but, this was their plan, and we had to trust they had picked the best alternative for our vacation.

This family meeting always ended the same way: my mom would ask us to put together a list of things we felt the need to bring with us: clothes, shoes, swimming gears, bikes, toys, snacks, etc.

The next Saturday, we had a follow-up meeting for us to present our wish lists. My parents would listen to us, suggest, recommend and provide us constructive feedback on the items we selected. By the end of our second family meeting, our list was revised and finalized.

And as always, our parents were the ones making the final decision. They were however giving us a little latitude to bring a couple of additional items – assuming there was sufficient space in our car.

The next days, and pending our departure, my brother and I had only two duties:
1. Pack all the items listed in the revised and agreed list
2. Ensure our rooms were spotless before departing on vacation

Through our yearly family vacations, and my parents' organizational skills, I learned important lessons that I am proud of carrying on and now share with my kids.
1. I already mentioned the first one: **everything we do can be considered as a project**
2. Good **project managers know when and how to engage all project stakeholders**
3. **Before embarking into any new ventures, we must be well-prepared.**

If you are reading this, you must already have set your mind into passing your Project Management Certification, but you may look for recommendations and tips on how to be successful at your first try. Interestingly enough, the Project Management Institute does not publish the actual success rate nor the passing score to the PMP Exam.

Nevertheless, we know that 75% is a key number:

- If you answer correctly 75% of questions of each process group, then there is a high probability of chance that you will pass your certification
- About 75% of people taking the exam are successful.

But, don't get this number fooled you!

Passing your PMP Certification requires to be focused and spend the necessary time and efforts to study and practice.

Going back to my childhood story, even though my parents were excellent project managers, organizing our yearly vacations with perfection, providing my brother and me the opportunity to know ahead of time where we will be heading, and giving us the chance to participate into the planning activities of our family project, it does not mean that my parents would have been successful at passing a traveling guide certification without applying the same organizational structure they were using to ensure my brother and I's participation and happiness.

It is my belief that the individuals who apply themselves to solve a problem can find the solution; that when you put the time and effort to improve your life, you can reach your personal and professional short-term goals; and once you have adopted a structured routine with the philosophy of continuous improvement, you then can achieve your long-term objectives.

It is also my strong belief and personal experience that **by following the 3-By-5 Steps Methodology, in 2 months, you can pass your PMP Certification!** But, instead of telling you more about it, let me simply present you the steps I recommend.

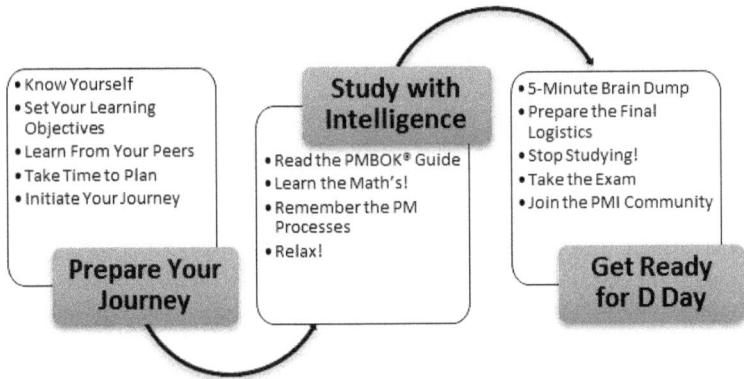

Prepare Your Journey
- Know Yourself
- Set Your Learning Objectives
- Learn From Your Peers
- Take Time to Plan
- Initiate Your Journey

Study with Intelligence
- Read the PMBOK® Guide
- Learn the Math's!
- Remember the PM Processes
- Relax!

Get Ready for D Day
- 5-Minute Brain Dump
- Prepare the Final Logistics
- Stop Studying!
- Take the Exam
- Join the PMI Community

1 Prepare Your Journey

When my parents were asking my brother and I to list all the things we wanted to bring with us during our yearly 2-week summer vacation, they were in fact asking us to prepare ourselves for our upcoming journey.

Similarly, the first phase of the 3-By-5 Steps to pass your PMP Certification is meant to assist you in getting ready for taking up and overcoming this new challenge in front of you.

Why preparing yourself? Why not jumping directly into the topic of Project Management?

Because, let's be realist: when was the last time you study to take an exam?

If you have the same background and experience as I do, when I decided to pass my PMP Certification, several years had passed since my graduation. I had forgotten how challenging it was to study academically. When I indeed decided to pass my PMP certification, it was more than 20 years after graduating, and naturally, with the exception of a couple of professional trainings and some continuous education classes, I had forgotten what it took to study and pass an exam.

In our daily life, personal and professional, countless times, we have demonstrated our abilities to learn new things and put them into practice. However, theoretical and practical learnings are two different animals!

So, be prepared!

The journey you are about to embark yourself is not an easy road. It requires your absolute commitment. And if you do commit, the 2-month long journey I propose you to follow will guide you through a successful outcome. Naturally, to emphasize this one last time, you must decide to make the necessary arrangements in your daily life to set aside the time to achieve your goal.

Simply put: **setting time aside requires preparation**.

This first phase is divided into the 5 following steps:
1. Know Yourself
2. Set Your Learning Objectives
3. Learn From Your Peers
4. Take Time to Plan Your Studies
5. Initiate Your Journey

Step #1: Know Yourself

In early 2006, I traveled for the first time in my life down to New Zealand to teach an introductory class on project management to a group of talented IT people. Arriving in Christchurch on Saturday afternoon, I was both exhausted and excited; exhausted by my obviously too long travels, and excited in meeting a brand new customer for the organization I was working for at the time.

The training was scheduled for five days and had been customized to satisfy the training requirements of this particular client. Working closely with my counterpart, three weeks prior to the first scheduled training class, I developed a curriculum that was meant to cover exactly what they wanted to focus on: this client indeed wanted to not only refresh the knowledge of his Senior IT Management staff on the fundamentals of project management but, to learn on how to better apply the Agile Scrum software development methodology to its already existing project management best practices.

Thus, on Monday morning, having somehow recuperated from the jet lag, I was excited to meet the trainees, and tackle this first day. More importantly, I was looking forward to unveiling to my counterpart and the attendees the final version of this week program. Needless to say, I was not expected such interesting reactions!

After the usual meet and greet, and going through a couple of ice-breakers to energize the room, I started presenting the agenda for the week: no reaction. A quick survey of the room, they all seemed ok. However, as soon as I presented today's agenda, right away, I noticed my counterpart's eyebrows frown; not a good sign when the day is so young. Nevertheless, I continued going over the agenda's slide and, moved on the next one: *"The 3-By-5 Steps Methodology Overview."*

Since my counterpart's eyebrows remained frown, I decided to ask her naively if there was a problem and she said *"yes,"* with a clearly disappointed tone, then adding that she did not fly me to New Zealand to talk about something so obvious than *"knowing yourself."* I was surprised by her so straightforward reaction, but I was not so surprised. Amazingly, it was not the first time someone asked me the exact same question.

That day, my answer was and has always been the same.

As simple as it may sound, the first step in learning something new, in changing anything we do in life, is to know who we are and understand our own drivers, our motivation to acquire a new skill, take up new challenge, to desire more, or reduce our wants.

Trust me, this is not an easy step!

We first must be truthful to ourselves since it's challenging to look with objectivity into our own mirror.

To know ourselves is to be aware of our own strengths and weaknesses.

It's the ability to observe and notice our reactions, moods, and responses to what is happening around us, and to understand how our emotions affect our state of mind.

To know ourselves is to comprehend how our environment may affect our mindset, and how we interact with others in various situations and state of mind.

It's the ability to be honest about our likes and dislikes, our wants and needs.

Knowing yourself is being capable of answering the following:

Who Are You?

This *"who"* question might sound silly as you have lived with yourself since the day you were born and, most certainly, you are the person who knows you best. And, if you have recently gone through or are in the process of preparing job interviews, you should have no issue answering the *"who."*

But, can you honestly and on-the-spot describe who you are in a couple of sentences?

For example, if I had to define my professional me, I would say the following:

> I am a Certified Senior Project Manager, who enjoys leading teams through challenging transformational, strategic or technical engagements. I excel in what I do when I am given the chance to work with diverse and creative people. And, last but not least, while being a very logical, and detailed-oriented person, I am also an out-of-the-box thinker who analyzes risks and opportunities using a top-down approach.

There are many sample answers online but, here are a few ones that may be more relevant to you, especially if you are or plan on becoming a project manager:

1. I'm an efficient and highly organized project manager. This enables me to manage several active projects in parallel, without overlooking any potential risks or issues.
2. I am someone who has a very pragmatic approach to solving problems, and I don't waste time talking about theory or the latest buzz words. My motivation and objective are clear: getting the job done within the project boundaries: scope, time, budget, while ensuring the satisfaction of my customers.
3. I always has an eye on my target, and figure out how to best collaborate with cross-functional teams to deliver high-quality work on time, on budget, every time.
4. With years of relevant experience in this industry, I am most certainly the most qualified project manager to take up the

challenges - people, process and technical challenges – that this transformational initiative entail.

5. I am a project manager who adapts his leadership style and methodology to the given situation. I thrive in an agile environment where I can transform obstacles into stepping stones for achievements.

6. As a software developer, I not only loved working as a team-player but, I demonstrated countless times that I always strive to bring the best out of the people, and do what I think is best for the company. As a project manager, I believe that I can apply my software engineering background and expertise to provide added value and benefits to the company.

7. I understand the complexity of the project management discipline. It's not just about creating a schedule and a plan. It's getting everyone to work together, collaboratively, and to agree on the best approach to move forward and meet the customer's needs and satisfactions, while maintain a constant eye on the overall project budget and profit margin.

Exercise: I am…

Try answering the following questions:

- Tell me about yourself; How would you describe yourself?
- What is your greatest strength?
- What is your greatest weakness?

I am: _____

_____

_____

_____

_____

_____

_____

My Greatest Strength is:

_____

_____

_____

_____

_____

_____

_____

My Greatest Weakness is:

_____

_____

_____

_____

_____

_____

_____

In addition to being capable of answering the "who," I have found critical to better know my own personality, my natural style, and my comfort zone. There are many tools you can use to get an objective assessment of your primary personality traits. The most notorious one is probably the Myers-Briggs Type Indicator, or MBTI.

According to our friends at Wikipedia, the Myers-Briggs Type Indicator assessment is a psychometric questionnaire designed to measure psychological preferences in how people perceive the world and make decisions.

Fundamentally, the Myers-Briggs Type Indicator is the theory of psychological type as originally developed by Carl Jung, who proposed the existence of two dichotomous pairs of cognitive functions:
- The "*rational*" (Judging) functions: Thinking and Feeling
- The "*irrational*" (Perceiving) functions: Sensation and Intuition

Leveraging Jung's work, Briggs and Myers developed their own theory on which the MBTI is based: Individuals are either born with, or develop, certain preferred ways of perceiving and deciding. The MBTI sorts some of these psychological differences into four opposite pairs, or dichotomies, with a resulting 16 possible psychological types.

None of these types are better or worse; however, Briggs and Myers theorized that individuals naturally prefer one overall combination of type differences. In the same way that writing with the left hand is hard work for a right-hander, so people tend to find using their opposite psychological preferences more difficult, even if they can become more proficient with practice and development.

The 16 types are typically referred to by an abbreviation of four letters - the initial letters of each of their four type preferences (except in the case of intuition, which uses the abbreviation N to distinguish it from introversion).

For instance:
- ESTJ: extraversion (E), sensing (S), thinking (T), judgment (J)
- INFP: introversion (I), intuition (N), feeling (F), perception (P)

The MBTI test is scored by evaluating each answer in terms of what it reveals about the test taker. Each question is relevant to one of the following cognitive learning styles.

Each cognitive learning style is not a polar opposite, but a gradual continuum.

- **Attitudes: Extraversion/Introversion (E/I):** The first continuum reflects what generically energizes a person. Extraverted types learn best by talking and interacting with others. By interacting with the physical world, extraverts can process and make sense of new information. Introverted types prefer quiet reflection and privacy. Information processing occurs for introverts as they explore ideas and concepts internally.

- **Functions: Sensing/Intuition (S/N):** The second continuum reflects what a person focuses their attentions on. Sensing types enjoy a learning environment in which the material is presented in a detailed and sequential manner. Sensing types often attend to what is occurring in the present, and can move to the abstract after they have established a concrete experience. Intuitive types prefer a learning atmosphere in which an emphasis is placed on meaning and associations. Insight is valued higher than careful observation, and pattern recognition occurs naturally for Intuitive types.

- **Functions: Thinking/Feeling (T/F):** The third continuum reflects the person's decision preferences. Thinking types desire objective truth and logical principles and are natural at deductive reasoning. Feeling types place an emphasis on issues and causes that can be personalized while they consider other people's motives.

- **Lifestyle: Judging/Perception (J/P):** The fourth continuum reflects how the person regards complexity. Judging types will thrive when information is organized and structured, and they will be motivated to complete assignments to gain closure. Perceiving types will flourish in a flexible learning environment in which they are stimulated by new and exciting ideas.

The below diagram[1] represent the Cognitive Functions:

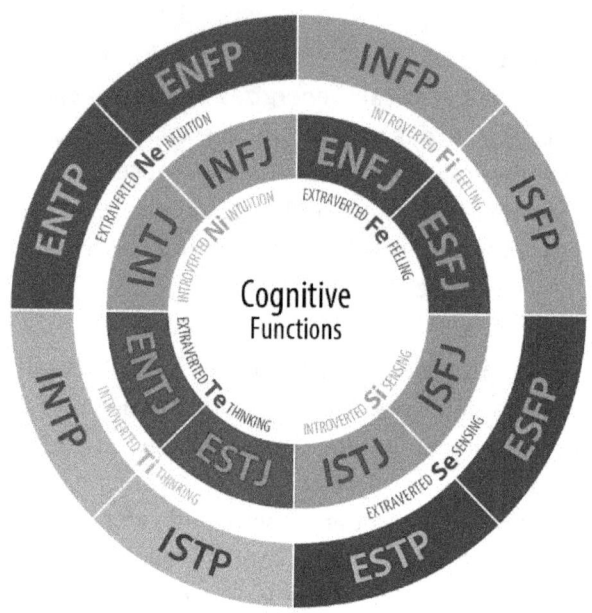

If you would like to take the MBTI test, you can visit the Myers-Briggs foundation at http://www.myersbriggs.org.

---

[1] The Cognitive Functions diagram is authored by Jake Beech, and licensed under the Creative Commons Zero, Public Domain Dedication via Wikimedia Commons

What Do You Want?

Let's go back to my childhood story and the yearly summer vacation my parents were so keen in making happened. After all the preparatory activities, my parents, brother and I were all taking place into our old Fiat, driving toward our vacation's location. However, even though we were all sitting in the same car, our wants going to our destination were different:

- My brother and I wanted to discover a new place, meet new friends, go to sleep as late as possible, and play all day in the sun
- My parents wanted to relax, and spend quality time with us

In other words, we had different wants, but the resulting immediate activity was the same.

You may want in the next ten years become the Director of your company's Project Management Office, and your coworker may be interested in changing career path to become a project manager. But concretely, you both are going to implement the same immediate step: passing your PMP Certification.

As explained in the previous section, knowing who we are is a key foundational element to our success in everything we do in life: if we know our strengths, weaknesses, and natural personality traits, then, we are closer to understand what we should do next to achieve our long term outcome... And, yes, this means that we must know what we want, or at the very least, know what we think we want for ourselves, for our loved ones, for our family, and for our friends.

So, let me ask you, what do you think you want to be or achieve in the next 10 to 20 years?

If you can't answer in a few seconds, don't worry. Unless you have already spent a considerable amount of time to think about this question, and put down on paper your thoughts, it should not surprise you.

First, we must make the difference between a need and a want. Not to quote the well-known Maslow's hierarchy of needs, and to keep it short and sweet, let me simply say the following:

- A need is something you have to have.
- A want is something you would like to have.

That being said, let's now focus on defining long term objectives; setting personal or professional lifetime goals is a complex exercise. It requires us to consider the unknowns, face our fear and dreams to think about what we want to achieve in our lifespan, what we want to leave behind, and what we want to be remembered for.

Understanding our lifetime goals may not be important today, but, tomorrow, when we would consider switching job, purchasing a new house, committing to study for a few months to pass a certification, or making any type of life-changing decision, these lifetime goals will be essential. Indeed, knowing how our immediate next step fit in the overall perspective of our life will shape all other aspects of our decision-making process. It helps separate the important from the non-important, and decide to move forward or discard an immediate step we may have originally thought was our best option.

Since you have purchased this book, it is fair to assume that you have most likely already defined your next step: passing the PMP Certification. But, does it make sense to you?

Passing the PMP Certification might appear today as the most logical and efficient next step in your professional career, but if your lifetime objective is to become a Cloud Computing technical expert, a Big Data guru, a Chief Finance Officer, or a renowned violist, I strongly recommend you not to embark into this project management journey.

Why? Because your motivation, personal and professional inner-drivers would simply not be aligned with this immediate next step: Passing the PMP Certification would not get you closer from your long-term goals. Hence, instead, focus and spend your time on achieving your lifelong goals: read the latest news and development on cloud computing, register to communities and forums related to Big Data, enroll in an MBA program, or train several hours a day playing violin.

On the other hand, if passing the PMP Certification is a natural step in your long-term career, stop doubting yourself! Be confident, and commit your time!

Exercise: I want...

Let's go one step further, and try answering the following questions:
- What are your goals for the next two years?
- Where do you see yourself 5 years from now?
- What is your dream job?

Don't hesitate to use the tools and techniques discussed in the *PMBOK®* *Guide* to generate new ideas. Some techniques imply working with a group – such as the Delphi technique or brainstorming – but, you can still apply the concept of these techniques. For instance, use the *"individual brainstorming"* technique. This method includes free writing, free speaking, word association, and/or drawing a mind map. In fact, recent studies have shown that *"individual brainstorming"* may be more effective in idea-generation than group brainstorming...

My goals for the next 2 years are: _____

_____

_____

_____

_____

_____

_____

_____

I see myself in the next 5 years as: _____

_____

_____

_____

_____

_____

_____

_____

My dream job is: _____

_____

_____

_____

_____

_____

_____

_____

As a project manager who has or is currently studying the Project Management Body of Knowledge, you must already be familiar with the criticality of defining clear requirements. You should apply the same philosophy when setting your personal and professional goals, regardless if they are long-term, mid-term or short-term objectives.

More specifically, in our projects, often, we have to satisfy unclear, misleading or unexpressed requirements. As project manager, our responsibility is to work with the customer and/or project sponsor to refine these requirements so that they are SMART: Specific, Measurable, Attainable, Relevant, and Time-bound.

When setting our lifetime or short-term objectives, we must do our best defining SMART goals so that, we can validate and celebrate our achievements.

For example, instead of saying *"I want to run as many marathons as I can"* as a personal goal, it's more powerful to say "*I want to run 100 marathons before turning 50 years old.*" Obviously, this will only be attainable if I train hard and consistently, but when I turn 50 years, I will easily be able to tell if I have achieved or if I need to adjust my goal.

At last, when setting lifelong goals, don't forget this famous quote:

"If your dreams don't scare you, they're not big enough."

Why Do You Want What You Want?

Every summer, with my parents and brother, we were driving several hours to reach our destination. Sometimes, we were staying in hotels, bed & breakfast, or we were camping. As a kid, my favorite vacations were the ones we had to sleep in our tent. It was both scary and fun, but it was most importantly different.

Out of all our vacations, 1971's is definitively one that I will remember all my life. I was nine years old. My parents had decided that we were going to drive to Austria, several hundred miles away from home, two days of travel. Before going, my dad already told us that our road trip was going to be a little longer than usual, but he forgot an important detail: our old Fiat...

And so, a few hours in, our car decided to break down on the side of the highway. And, remember, back in 1971, there was no cellphone: My dad had therefore to leave us there, walk to the first village, find a payphone, and call for help. A couple of hours later, he was back with a tow truck. We stayed about half-a-day in Bologna, hoping our car would be fixed the next morning. Luckily, our car got repaired, and we were on our way the next day...

When we finally reached our campground, we didn't have to be Einstein to understand that my mom was not happy. She never liked camping... We still managed to spend a wonderful vacation, visiting the southern part of Austria, and swimming in the most spectacular lake I have ever seen; my only regret: not remembering the name of this lake...

That said, why my parents wanted us to go to Austria? What was their motivation to dive so far?

Looking back with my father's eyes, I can state with certitude that their motivation, their "why" was simple: They wanted to create amazing memories for all us to share. And for this sole reason, because of this key personal goal, my dad was willing to deal with the mechanical problems of our old car, and my mom to sleep a few days in an uncomfortable tent.

Knowing yourself is therefore being capable of answering the following three questions:

- Who are you?
- What do you want?
- Why do you want what you want?

Assuming all our needs are fulfilled, who we are (our strengths, weaknesses, likes and dislikes) drives our wants. Our wants should however be asserted by a clear reason: a motivation.

Why? Because without an undeniable motivator, a constant and persistent catalyst to draw all our energy toward our wants, we are most likely to fail. Motivation is the energy that drives us to accomplish our goals. And, we need motivation in huge doses and we need it daily to stay on track. It's too easy to give up when obstacles are thrown our ways; and trust me, in our route to success, to passing the PMP Certification, obstacles will be thrown our ways.

So, if you feel you are lacking motivation to go the extra-mile, and pass your certification, remember my favorite quotes from Thomas Edison:

"Many of life's failures are people who did not realize how close they were to success when they gave up."

"If we did all the things we are capable of doing, we would literally astound ourselves."

Do you now feel inspired?

Are you now motivated?

Exercise: I am motivated by....

The next questions you may want to answer are:

- What motivates you?
- Why do you wish to pass your PMP Certification?

I am motivated by: _____

_____

_____

_____

_____

_____

_____

I want to pass the PMP certification because: _____

_____

_____

_____

_____

_____

_____

What's Your Mission Statement?

A mission statement defines the purpose of a company or person, and its reason for existing. A mission statement is meant at guiding the actions of the organization, spelling out its overall goal, providing a path, and guiding the decision-making process.

Based on my (personal and professional) experiences, being able to articulate our own mission statement is critical during tough times. It reminds us why we are doing what we do, why we have decided to embark into a challenging journey, why we have committed so much time in achieving a goal.

A personal mission statement indeed provides us clarity and gives us a sense of purpose to achieve a particular outcome: Passing the Project Management Professional Certification. It helps us in understanding the larger picture, the reason why we have decided to spend a couple of months of our lives studying the project management discipline.

It may sound a little ridiculous to write a mission statement for ourselves. However, the highest performers view themselves as self-employed and often have the attitude of entrepreneurs running their own business, even if they work for a company. With such attitude, they develop a sense of *"mission"* about their career, and take a proactive approach to create the results they want. For examples, Denise Morrison (CEO of Campbell Soup Company), Joel Mandy (CEO of Herschend Family Entertainment), Sir Richard Branson (founder of The Virgin Group), Oprah Winfrey (founder of OWN, the Oprah Winfrey Network) all have defined their own personal mission statement:

- Denise Morrison: "To serve as a leader, live a balanced life, and apply ethical principles to make a significant difference."
- Joel Manby: *"I define personal success as being consistent to my own personal mission statement: to love God and love others."*
- Sir Richard Branson: *"To have fun in [my] journey through life and learn from [my] mistakes."*
- Oprah Winfrey: *"To be a teacher. And to be known for inspiring my students to be more than they thought they could be."*

Thus, before moving forward to our next step (Set Your Learning Objectives), taking into consideration the three previous questions and related answers, you should be able to define your mission statement!

Exercise: My mission is...

Keeping in mind your current goal (passing the PMP Certification), and using the following steps, write your Personal Mission Statement:

1. Review the answers of previous questions (who, what and why)
2. Write a short paragraph describing why you want to pass the PMP Certification
3. Include a specific and measurable studying outcomes
4. Define a deadline to pass your exam
5. Write your Mission Statement

It is my mission to: _____

_____

_____

_____

_____

_____

_____

Once you are satisfied with your Personal Mission Statement, my recommendation is to print and mount it in your bedroom, office, and anywhere you plan on studying for the project management discipline. This will remind you constantly why you are walking on this grueling road to the PMP certification.

Step #2: Set Your Learning Objectives

In Step #1, we articulated the reason why you want to become a Certified Project Manager. And, now that you are armed with your own personal motivators, and are committed to take up this two-month journey and pass successfully your certification, we can start thinking about the immediate next step: Setting Your Learning Objectives.

What Are Your Project Management Strengths?

More specifically, in this step, we are going to assist you in identifying the project management knowledge areas and processes you may need to first focus on. The *PMBOK® Guide* Fifth Edition defines five process groups and ten knowledge areas.

The five process groups are:
1. Initiating
2. Planning
3. Executing
4. Monitoring and Controlling
5. Closing

The ten Knowledge Areas are:
4. Project Integration Management
5. Project Scope Management
6. Project Time Management
7. Project Cost Management
8. Project Quality Management
9. Project Human Resource Management
10. Project Communications Management
11. Project Risk Management
12. Project Procurement Management
13. Project Stakeholder Management

Each knowledge area is composed by a certain number of project management processes, with well-defined inputs and outputs that are produced through the use of specific tools and techniques. Because we all have different experiences managing projects, we begin this journey at a different starting point. Recognizing this simple fact implies that, even though our goal is the same – passing the PMP Certification - our learning objectives should naturally be different.

For example, when I personally decided to embark into this expedition, I knew I will be challenged by the cost and procurement management processes; in my professional career, I was indeed always able to count on talented financial controllers and a well-rounded procurement team. And so, when I started studying for the PMP, I knew I had to spend more time focusing on these two areas.

In this second step, we are therefore going to achieve two things:
   a) identify and bring awareness on the process groups and areas you may need to primarily focus on, or at the very least, spend a little bit more time on
   b) start drafting a high-level timeline for your journey

Exercise: I can assess my skills....

Vertically, the *PMBOK® Guide* classifies the Project Management Processes in five process groups, and horizontally, in ten knowledge areas. This first exercise consist in assessing your own experiences.

Let us focus on the Process Groups: Rate your experience performing the processes relevant to each process group, considering the following scale:
   1: you have no experience performing or supporting this set of processes
   2: you have performed or supported the execution of these processes on 1 project
   3: you have performed or supported the execution of these processes on at least 3 projects
   5: you have performed these processes on at least 5 projects
   7: you have performed these processes on at least 10 projects
   10: you have performed these processes on way too many projects; you are an expert.

Process Group	Process Group Description	Your Rating (1 to 10)
Initiating	Define a new project or a new phase of an existing project by obtaining authorization to start the project or phase	_____
Planning	Establish the scope of the project, refine the objectives, and define the course of action required to attain the objectives that the project was undertaken to achieve	_____
Executing	Complete the work defined in the project management plan to satisfy the project specifications	_____
Monitoring & Controlling	Track, review, and regulate the progress and performance of the project; identify any areas in which changes to the plan are required; and initiate the corresponding changes	_____
Closing	Finalize all activities across all Process Groups to formally close the project or phase	_____

Using the same scale, assess your experience in each Knowledge Areas defined in the *PMBOK® Guide*:

Knowledge Area	Knowledge Area Description	Your Rating (1 to 10)
4. Project Integration Management	Identify, define, combine, unify, and coordinate the various processes and management activities. Includes making choices about resource allocation, making trade-offs among competing objectives and alternatives, and managing the interdependencies among the project management Knowledge Areas.	_____

Knowledge Area	Knowledge Area Description	Your Rating (1 to 10)
5. Project Scope Management	Ensure that the project includes all the work required, and only the work required, to complete the project successfully. Define and control what is and is not included in the project.	_____
6. Project Time Management	Manage the timely completion of the project. Define, sequence, estimate, and control the project activities and schedule.	_____
7. Project Cost Management	Plan, estimate, budget, finance, fund, manage, and control costs so that the project can be completed within the approved budget.	_____
8. Project Quality Management	Determine quality policies, objectives, and responsibilities so that the project will satisfy the needs. Ensure that the project requirements, including product requirements, are met and validated.	_____
9. Project Human Resource Management	Organize, acquire, develop, manage, and lead the project team.	_____
10. Project Communications Management	Ensure timely and appropriate planning, collection, creation, distribution, storage, retrieval, management, control, monitoring, and the ultimate disposition of project information. Include internal (at all organizational levels) and external communications (external to the organization).	_____
11. Project Risk Management	Conduct risk management planning, identification, qualitative and quantitative analysis. Plan risk response, and control risk on a project.	_____

Knowledge Area	Knowledge Area Description	Your Rating (1 to 10)
12. Project Procurement Management	Purchase or acquire products, services, or results needed from outside the project team. Plan and conduct procurements, and administer contracts or purchase orders.	_____
13. Project Stakeholder Management	Identify the people, groups, or organizations that could impact or be impacted by the project, to analyze stakeholder expectations and their impact on the project. Develop appropriate management strategies for effectively engaging stakeholders in project decisions and execution.	_____

At last, and please, don't be scared or worried, assess your comfort level regarding certain areas of mathematics; some project management processes indeed do leverage mathematics to be performed successfully, and the PMP Exam will not spare you!

But, like everything in life, if we are well-prepared, we can handle anything life throws at us…

Math's Area	Math's Area Description	Your Rating (1 to 10)
Arithmetic	Study of numbers and their traditional operations: addition, subtraction, multiplication, division. *Note:* During the PMP Exam, you will be able to use a calculator; however, my advice is not to use it: you will save critical minutes if you can perform the simple arithmetical operations in your mind.	_____
Elementary Algebra	Methods to solve polynomial equations with one or more unknown variables	_____

Math's Area	Math's Area Description	Your Rating (1 to 10)
Mathematical Analysis	Theory of differentiation, integration, measure, limits, infinite series, and analytic functions with real numbers	_____
Combinatory	Includes a) the study of discrete collections of objects satisfying specific criteria, and b) the graph theory (network, collection of connected points)	_____
Probability	Random variables, stochastic processes and events, distributions (continuous, normal, pareto, beta, triangular, etc.)	_____
Statistics	Study of collection, including sampling techniques, standard deviation, sigma, mean, mode, median, and range	_____

What Are Your Learning Objectives?

The rating obtained in the previous exercise should now help you in defining your personal learning objectives. Naturally, I want you to focus on the areas your rating is less. However, I don't want you to overlook the areas where you already excel in.

Please, remember the following: to pass the PMP Exam, you must be not only proficient in a couple of process groups, you must be proficient in most of them!

Our next immediate step consists in drafting a template for your own learning journey. As I introduced it earlier, everything we do in life can be considered as a project. Thus, you should think of this journey as your professional self-improvement project that has one clear goal: passing the PMP exam. And as any other projects, before kicking off any activities, and working on developing the various anticipated deliverables, we must draft a high-level plan.

Thus, the purpose of the template you are now going to build is aimed at become a foundational component, a key structural building block to your project, a high-level roadmap that we will be re-using in our next steps:

Step #3: Learn from Your Peers, and *Step #4: Take Time to Plan Your Studies*.

Exercise: My learning objectives are…

In the "*Exercise: I can assess my skills….*", you have tried to rate your own skills as objectively as possible, using the following scale:

1: you have no experience performing or supporting this set of processes

2: you have performed or supported the execution of these processes on 1 project

3: you have performed or supported the execution of these processes on at least 3 projects

5: you have performed these processes on at least 5 projects

7: you have performed these processes on at least 10 projects

10: you have performed these processes on way too many projects; you are an expert.

In this exercise, we are going to first prioritize the process groups, knowledge and mathematics areas. The prioritization is going to use percentage, as illustrated below.

Master the Project Management Discipline The Pass Module Step #2: Set Your Learning Objectives		Enter Your Assessment Ratings in this Column	
Process Group	Process Group Description	Your Rating (1 to 10)	Percentage
Initiating	define a new project or a new phase of an existing project by obtaining authorization to start the project or phase	5	22.02%
Planning	establish the scope of the project, refine the objectives, and define the course of action required to attain the objectives that the project was undertaken to achieve	6	18.35%
Executing	Complete the work defined in the project management plan to satisfy the project specifications	6	18.35%
Monitoring & Controlling	track, review, and regulate the progress and performance of the project; identify any areas in which changes to the plan are required; and initiate the corresponding changes	8	13.76%
Closing	finalize all activities across all Process Groups to formally close the project or phase	4	27.52%

The calculated percentages should help you define the time and effort to consider putting into each process group, knowledge area and applied mathematics. But, don't worry, we are not going to ask you to calculate these percentage manually; we are indeed inviting you to leverage one of the 3 accelerators (*Step#2 Accelerator*) offered on the ADVENCYS website at the following link: http://www.advencys.com/the3by5freebonus.html. This Accelerator is a Microsoft Excel spreadsheet.

You should now be able to assess with objectivity where you are, and which particular areas may require additional attention while studying for the PMP Certification. These areas are your primary learning objectives, while never forgetting the larger picture: even though you may be an expert in Time Management, you should not overlook this Knowledge Area.

Step #3: Learn From Your Peers

In the previous step, through self-assessment, we have defined our primary learning objectives to study for the Project Management Professional Certification. In this natural next step, we are going to inject into your defined objectives inputs from your peers.

Who can I learn from?

In *"Cognitive perspectives on peer learning,"* edited by Angela M. O'Donnell and Alison King, peer learning is defined as follows: *"Peer learning is an educational practice in which students interact with other students to attain educational goals."* Interacting and collaborating with our peers is the most efficient method to gain insights into the strengths and weaknesses, and into the PMP Exam.

Why? Because they know us, they are aware of our strengths and weaknesses, and because they may already have climbed the mountain, or tried to attain the summit we are now training to reach. So, even though we may not be ready to share with our coworkers our interest and ambition in passing the PMP Certification, or we may not feel comfortable asking about their own personal experience studying for and taking the PMP Exam, this is a necessary step.

However, as all other steps, we have options, and the technique I am now going to talk about should hopefully help you in achieving this third step. This technique is a well-establish one, dating from the 1950s: **the 360-degree feedback**.

The 360-degree feedback, also known as multi-source assessment, is feedback that comes from members of our immediate work circle. 360-degree feedback includes feedback from our employees (people we manage), peers (our colleagues), and supervisor(s), as well as a self-evaluation. The results from a 360-degree evaluation can then be used to plan and map our journey: **Step #4: Take Time to Plan Your Studies**.

Let's stop talking, and continue our 360-degree feedback! In the previous step: **Step #2: Set Your Learning Objectives,** we complete our self-assessment; one thing done!

Exercise: I am going to ask feedback from...

The first thing we need to do is to identify the people we would like to get feedback from.

They fall under 3 categories: employees (people we manage), peers (our colleagues), and managers. But, who are they? Who do you know has tried to or successfully passed their PMP Certification?

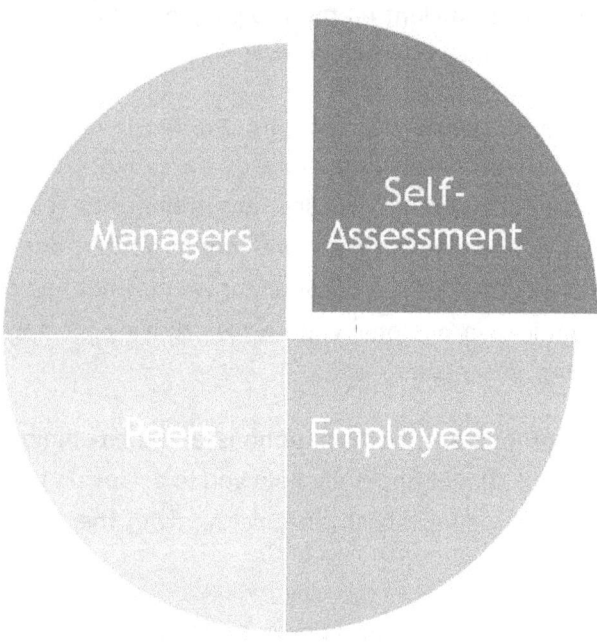

I am going to ask feedback from the following Employees: _____

_____

_____

_____

I am going to ask feedback from my following Peers: _____

_____

_____

_____

I am going to ask feedback from the following Managers: _____

_____

_____

_____

How should I conduct 360-degree feedback?

Now, we are almost ready to conduct this 360-degree feedback. But, before kicking-off this exercise, let's set some ground rules:

1. Keep in mind the purpose of this 360-degree feedback:
   a. Gain additional insights into the PMP Exam
   b. Listen to what your interlocutor has to say about the areas you may want to focus on
2. Schedule a meeting with your interlocutors
3. Communicate the purpose this 360-degree feedback
4. Time-box the discussions to 30 minutes maximum
5. Prepare the questions you are going to ask about the areas you may need to focus on
6. Be ready and accept any negative and constructive feedback
7. Ask opened questions regarding the PMP Exam itself
8. Don't request feedback from 30 people: keep it small!

It's now time to jump into the ocean, and swim!

Exercise: My 360-degree feedback highlighted...

My Employees recommended me to: _____

_____

_____

_____

_____

_____

_____

My Peers recommended me to: _____

_____

_____

_____

_____

_____

_____

_____

My Managers recommended me to: _____

_____

_____

_____

_____

_____

_____

_____

The feedback you have gathered through this 360-degree feedback exercise should normally confirm the results of your self-assessment, and, further refine the ratings you documented in the Step #2 Spreadsheet. Before moving forward into our journey, I recommend you to update these ratings based on the results of the 360-degree assessment.

The more accurate and objective you are, the better position you will be in, to tackle the next step...

Step #4: Take Time to Plan Your Studies

As explained earlier, **everything we do in life can be defined as a project**; this journey to pass the PMP Certification is no different. Thus far, we have a well-defined goal, and a drafted scope of work. This fourth step is aimed at guiding us through the definition of last 2 dimensions of our personal and professional self-improvement project: estimate the time and costs.

Let us start by estimating the direct costs associated with our commitment.

How much will my PMP Certification project cost?

According to our Wikipedia's friends, costs that are directly attributable to the object are direct costs. In construction, the costs of materials, labor, equipment, etc., and all directly involved efforts or expenses for the cost object are direct costs. Direct costs are those for activities or services that benefit specific projects, for example salaries for project staff and materials required for a particular project.

In our case, in our journey to pass the PMP Certification, since we are all volunteered, there is no salary to consider. On the other hand, we must consider the costs associated with the necessary training materials (including this book), and the registration fees to the exam, etc.

Having a good understanding of high-level costs of any projects is critical: any person and organization must consider carefully the costs associated with potential initiatives, simply asking if it's worth investigating into the project: Am I going to benefit from the project? Will my organization increase its revenue, reputation, or gain additional market share?

This may sound like a puzzling and tricky task to achieve, especially if we have just started thinking about possibly taking the PMP Exam. That being said, on the positive side, the direct costs to take the PMP exam is very well documented by the Project Management Institute. Thus, when it comes to the costs related to the exam itself, we can very easily estimate with accuracy and precision our costs – the next paragraphs describe these costs. The variable part of our journey direct costs is the training materials – the next exercise will guide us in estimating these variable training costs.

The Project Management Institute provides all the information we need to understand the process for applying to the PMP Certification, and estimate the associated costs, on the PMI website: http://www.pmi.org/Certification/Project-Management-Professional-PMP.aspx.

The PMP handbook also provides great details regarding the costs. The PMP handbook is available for free on the PMI website at: http://www.pmi.org/certification/~/media/pdf/certifications/pdc_pmphandbook.ashx.

The next paragraph summarizes the costs of exam as of September 2014.

As explained earlier, most candidates take the PMP Exam as a Computer Based Testing (CBT). The registration fee is US $555 for non-PMI members and US $405 for PMI members.

Before applying, my recommendation is to become a PMI member (US $129 to join and US $10 for the application). By joining, you will indeed save on the training materials you will need; as a PMI member, you can download the *PMBOK® Guide* along with many other PMI publications for free. Not only you will reduce the cost of your professional improvement project, you will also be able to connect with other members who have the same objectives.

Exercise: My estimated costs are...

As you must already know, there are many books, software training solutions, online and traditional classroom trainings available to us. But what would work best for you? Are you an avid reader? Are you more effective when you are alone? Do you learn faster by listening and sharing ideas with others? Do you need to focus on your soft skills? Do you want to learn more about the technical tools of project management?

Answering these questions is essential if you would like to choose and pick the tools that will work for you.

But, let's move on, and estimate your training direct costs.

The Books I am interested in reading are: _____

_____

_____

_____

_____

_____

The Software Training Solutions I am interested in leveraging are:

_____

_____

_____

_____

The Online Training Classes I am interested in registering are:

_____

_____

_____

_____

_____

The Traditional Training Classes I am interested in attending are:

_____

_____

_____

_____

Note: When considering an online or traditional classroom training, I strongly advise you to go through a PMI Registered Education Provider. PMI R.E.P.s are organizations that the Project Management Institute has approved to offer training in project management and issue professional development units (PDUs) to meet the continuing education requirements needed by PMI credential holders. To search for a R.E.P, you can use the PMI website: http://www.pmi.org/en/Professional-Development/REP-Find-a-Registered-Education-Provider.aspx.

Next is to add the individual estimated costs...

Training Material	Estimated Cost

Estimated Total Training Costs:	

Note: If you plan on leveraging books from the Project Management Institute, consider becoming a PMI member; as a member, the cost of these books may be free or be considerably discounted.

How long will my PMP Certification project take?

Now that you have a good understanding of the direct costs to pass the PMP certification, including registration fees and training materials, the natural next step is to estimate how long your PMP Certification project will take.

Thinking like project managers, to do any sort of estimations, we must first define the various tasks we must perform; in other words, we must define the Work Breakdown Structure (WBS) of our journey. A Work Breakdown Structure is a deliverable-oriented decomposition of a project into smaller components; components that are manageable and can be estimated. Thus, a WBS provides us the required framework to perform detailed time and cost estimating.

Since we are applying this 3-By-5 Process Improvement Methodology to reach our destination, and taking into consideration the outputs of the three first steps, why don't we leverage the 3-By-5 Steps to develop the Work Breakdown Structure of our journey.

This WBS can be illustrated as depicted in the next page table:

Task ID	Task Name	Start Date	LoE in Day	End Date	Predecessor	Successor
1	The 3-By-5 Steps: To Pass Your PMP Certification	09/03/2014	61	01/03/2015	N/A	N/A
1.1	1: Prepare Your Journey	11/03/2014	13	11/16/2014	N/A	N/A
1.1.1	Step #1: Know Yourself	11/03/2014	2	11/05/2014	N/A	1.1.2
1.1.2	Step #2: Set Your Learning Objectives	11/05/2014	3	11/08/2014	1.1.1	1.1.3
1.1.3	Step #3: Learn From Your Peers	11/08/2014	3	11/11/2014	1.1.2	1.1.4
1.1.4	Step #4: Take Time to Plan Your Studies	11/11/2014	3	11/14/2014	1.1.3	1.1.5
1.1.5	Step #5: Initiate Your Journey	11/14/2014	2	11/16/2014	1.1.4	1.2.6.1
1.2	2: Study With Intelligence	11/16/2014	40	12/26/2014	N/A	N/A
1.2.6	Step #6: Read PMBOK® Guide, Fifth Edition	11/16/2014	24	12/10/2014	N/A	N/A
1.2.6.1	Introduction	11/16/2014	0.5	11/16/2014	1.1.5	1.2.6.2
1.2.6.2	Organizational Influences and Project Life Cycles	11/16/2014	0.5	11/17/2014	1.2.6.1	1.2.6.3
1.2.6.3	Project Management Processes	11/17/2014	1	11/18/2014	1.2.6.2	1.2.6.4
1.2.6.4	Project Integration Management	11/18/2014	1	11/19/2014	1.2.6.3	1.2.6.5
1.2.6.5	Project Scope Management	11/19/2014	2	11/21/2014	1.2.6.4	1.2.6.6
1.2.6.6	Project Time Management	11/21/2014	3	11/24/2014	1.2.6.5	1.2.6.7
1.2.6.7	Project Cost Management	11/24/2014	3	11/27/2014	1.2.6.6	1.2.6.8
1.2.6.8	Project Quality Management	11/27/2014	3	11/30/2014	1.2.6.7	1.2.6.9
1.2.6.9	Project Human Resource Management	11/30/2014	1	12/01/2014	1.2.6.8	1.2.6.10
1.2.6.10	Project Communication Management	12/01/2014	1	12/02/2014	1.2.6.9	1.2.6.11
1.2.6.11	Project Risk Management	12/02/2014	2	12/04/2014	1.2.6.10	1.2.6.12
1.2.6.12	Project Procurement Management	12/04/2014	2	12/06/2014	1.2.6.11	1.2.6.13
1.2.6.13	Project Stakeholder Management	12/06/2014	2	12/08/2014	1.2.6.12	1.2.6.X3
1.2.6.X3	Interpersonal Skills	12/08/2014	1	12/09/2014	1.2.6.13	1.2.6.CE
1.2.6.CE	PMI Code of Ethics and Professional Conduct	12/09/2014	1	12/10/2014	1.2.6.X3	1.2.7
1.2.7	Step #7: Learn the Math's	12/10/2014	3	12/13/2014	1.2.6.CE	1.2.8
1.2.8	Step #8: Remember the Project Management Processes	12/13/2014	2	12/15/2014	1.2.7	1.2.9
1.2.9	Step #9: Simulate the PMP® Exam	12/15/2014	10	12/25/2014	1.2.8	1.2.10
1.2.10	Step #10: Don't Forget to Relax	12/25/2014	1	12/26/2014	1.2.9	1.3.11
1.3	3: Get Ready for Day D	12/26/2014	8	12/29/2014	N/A	N/A
1.3.11	Step #11: Train For a 5-Minute Brain Dump	12/26/2014	3	12/29/2014	1.2.10	1.3.12
1.3.12	Step #12: Prepare the Final Logistics	12/29/2014	2	12/31/2014	1.3.11	1.3.13
1.3.13	Step #13: Stop Studying and Sleep Well	12/31/2014	1	01/01/2015	1.3.12	1.3.14
1.3.14	Step #14: Start Your Exam with Confidence	01/01/2015	1	01/02/2015	1.3.13	1.3.15
1.3.15	Step #15: Join the PMI Community	01/02/2015	1	01/03/2015	1.3.14	2
2	The 3-By-5 Steps: To Manage Projects	01/03/2015			1.3.15	

Enter the date you
would like to take
the PMP Exam

As illustrated in the above WBS, our estimated level of efforts to complete this journey is 61 days.

Nevertheless, as mentioned earlier, we all come into this journey with different experience managing projects and, in consequence, we all start at a different point. You may feel that a 61 day journey is too long or too short based on your existing knowledge of project management discipline. And you are right! The proposed 61-day journey is not a prescription to follow to the letter. It is simply a starting point for you to leverage in your own planning exercise.

Exercise: My estimated timeline is...

In the previous steps, we completed a self-assessment of your project management experience and knowledge. We revised the results of the self-assessment by performing 360-degree review with a selected group of employees, peers and managers, identifying and defining our own learning objectives. Taking into considerations these inputs, and leveraging the 3-By-5 Work Breakdown Structure, we can assert with confidence that we can start planning the reminder of this project.

This estimation exercise consists of:

1. Download the Step#4 Accelerator on the ADVENCYS website at the following link: http://www.advencys.com/the3by5.html
   This Accelerator is a Microsoft Excel spreadsheet.
2. Define the *target date* you would like to take the PMP Exam
3. Locate the Start Date of **Step #14: Start Your Exam with Confidence**
4. Enter the *target date* you have defined
5. Locate the Level of Effort (LoE) column for the **Step #6: Read the *PMBOK® Guide* subtasks**
6. For each subtasks of **Step #6: Read the *PMBOK® Guide***, using the 360-Degree feedback ratings, update as appropriate the associated level of efforts
7. Save the Spreadsheet

Note: if the Start Date of "The 3-By-5 Steps: To Pass Your PMP Certification" task shows in red, you will not reach your destination with confidence; consider moving the *target date* to a later date, thus giving you the necessary and sufficient time to study.

Step #5: Initiate Your Journey

If I may, allow me one last time to tell you about my childhood and the yearly family 2-week summer vacation my parents were so adamant to organize for my older brother and I.

When I was growing up, and until I left my parents' hometown, it was a tradition for my Dad and my Mom to organize and hold a family meeting two weeks prior to the beginning of our 2-week vacation. This family meeting had three objectives:

1. Tell us about the plan, listen to my brother and I's concerns and suggestions, and ensure our full commitment in the final preparation of upcoming vacations,
2. Set a target departure date (i.e. a clear deadline) for us to work towards to, and
3. Set the plan in motion

My brother and I knew that my parents spent countless hours defining where we were going to spend our vacation. They looked at maps, searched the phonebook for restaurants, hotels, campgrounds, and activities we could do. They had to call many people and, made all the necessary reservations. Trust me, planning a 2-week vacation was not an easy task, especially since we did not have this incredibly powerful spider web that we now call Internet.

And as you go through your project management career, you will learn very fast the simple fact that planning is challenging. However, a project plan is only a plan, an idea that has been further refined and vetted through a various set of tools and techniques. And a plan will always only be plan until we decide to move forward, and start executing!

So, why don't we initiate this journey?

After all, we have a robust plan. We have done our due diligences, assessed objectively where we are, and discussed and understood where we need to go.

Does it mean we know everything? Absolutely not! But, will we know more about what we don't know if we continue planning some more? Perhaps, but we will certainly not uncover all unknowns hidden under the rocks, and we need to accept this fact.

Let's be honest with ourselves: initiating a plan, giving the go decision to any projects, is a risk, and is also an amazing opportunity!

As a person, or as an organization, we must recognize this reality. And with the right tools and techniques, we can mitigate risks, and optimize opportunities.

So, tell me: are you ready?

Are you ready to apply to and schedule your PMP exam?

How do I apply for the PMP exam?

The Project Management Institute has published a comprehensive handbook guiding the candidates to the PMP Exam. This handbook provides an overview of the PMP Credential, the PMP Application and Payment, the Credential Examination Policies and Procedures, as well as discusses how you can use your PMI Credentials. This handbook is available for free on the PMI website at:

http://www.pmi.org/certification/~/media/pdf/certifications/pdc_pmphandbook.ashx.

The next exercise helps you gather the information you need when applying for the PMP Exam.

Exercise: I am ready to apply…

To apply for the PMP Exam, there are requirements; you need to have:

- A secondary degree (high school diploma, associate's degree, or the global equivalent) with at least five years of project management experience, with 7,500 hours leading and directing projects and 35 hours of project management education.

OR

- A four-year degree (bachelor's degree or the global equivalent) and at least three years of project management experience, with 4,500 hours leading and directing projects and 35 hours of project management education.

To successfully applying for the PMP Exam, the PMI must be able to validate that you meet the perquisite requirements.

Completing the next tables will help you gather the information the PMI requests to provide during your online application. In particular, the Education and Training table will help you confirm that you have the prerequisite diploma/degree, and that you have completed the required 35 hours of project management training.

Education and Training	
Highest Degree:	
Year degree was awarded:	
Name of High School, College or University:	
Address of High School, College or University:	
Completed Project Management Training	*You must have 35 hours of project management education / training to meet the PMP Exam application's prerequisite requirements.* *As need be, you may refer to several completed training.*
Course Title:	
Institute:	

Category (A – F):	A: PMI Registered Education Providers (R.E.P.s) B: Courses or Programs offered by PMI Chapters or communities of practice C: Employer/Company-Sponsored programs D: Training companies or consultants E: Distance-Learning companies, including an end of course assessment F: University/College academic and continuing education programs
Total Hours:	
Qualifying Hours:	

The Project Experience will help you confirm that you have the mandatory project management experiences.

Project Experience				
Project	Depending on your highest degree, you must demonstrate to the PMI that you have either 7,500 hours or 4,500 hours leading and directing projects. You will also be asked how many hours you have spent performing each project management process groups. As need be, you may refer to several projects.			
Project Title:				
Start/End Date:				
Project Role:				
Job Title:				
Organization Name:				
Organization Address:				
Organization Phone Number:				
Numbers of Hours Spent on each Process Groups				
Initiating	*Planning*	*Executing*	*Controlling*	*Closing*

What else? Nothing! Congratulations! You are ready to **Start Your Online Application** on the PMI website: https://certification.pmi.org.

After submitting your application, you still have to schedule your PMP Exam. This is your objective, the goal of your project. So **until you actually set the date of your PMP Exam, your project is not a project;** according to the *PMBOK® Guide, "a project is a temporary endeavor designed to produce a unique product, service or result with a defined beginning and end."* In other words, until you do define *"the end,"* until you set the date of your PMP Exam passing, based on my experience, it will be very challenging to find the necessary motivation and drivers to reach your objective.

That being said, since the PMI usually takes 5 days to process your application submitted online, we strongly recommend you not to wait for your application to be approved to initiate the rest of your journey; think parallel-tasking!

Step to the next phase, **Study with Intelligence**, start reading the *PMBOK® Guide*, and once your application is approved, once you will receive an email from the PMI, schedule your PMP Exam.

Exercise: I am approved, and ready to schedule my PMP Exam...

Once you have received the confirmation email from the PMI along with your **PMI Edibility ID**, you can set the date of your PMP Exam. As always, to do so, the Project Management Institute provides well-defined steps to follow on its website:

http://www.pmi.org/~/media/PDF/Certifications/CredentialExamScheduli ngInstructions.ashx.

To summarize these steps:
1. Go to the Prometric website: http://www.prometric.com/pmi
2. Under the section labeled *"I want to...,"* under the PMP Candidates section, select *"Schedule an Appointment"*
3. Select your geographical location from the dropdown menu, and click *"Next."*
4. Select *"Schedule an Appointment."*

5. Read through the examination information presented on your screen, and click "*Next*"
6. Read through and agree to the Policies and Data Privacy Notice
7. Enter your unique PMI Eligibility ID (the number ending with an "*E*" located on your scheduling notification) and the first four letters of your last name (as they appear on your government issued identification). Click "*Next*."
8. Use the tool provided to search for testing sites in your area. Select "*Schedule an Appointment*."
9. Locate and select your exam date and time. Available dates will appear in blue on the calendar, and dates with no appointments available will be in grey. Select your date from the calendar provided, and then your time. Click "*Next*."
10. Confirm your contact information and provide a valid email address. Please note, the email address provided will be the email that your examination confirmation will be sent to. Once your information is entered and confirmed, click "*Next*."
11. Review your final appointment details, and then click "*Complete Appointment*." Your appointment will not be scheduled until you click "*Complete Appointment*."

Your examination confirmation, along with your 16 digit unique confirmation number, will be displayed. This information will also be sent via email to the address provided.

Print and Keep this email! You will have to bring it with you the day of the exam.

At last, don't forget to change your plan if you could not schedule the PMP Exam at the date you defined in the previous step; as any project managers, maintaining the project plan is key to monitor and control the execution of project...

2   Study with Intelligence

Let's not fool ourselves; there is no magic bullet. There has never been one: only hard work will open the doors to the PMP Certification.

However, the next steps should assist in studying for the PMP Exam and be ready on D Day to shoot confidently our target with accuracy and precision. How? By refining our aim!

Have you ever fired a pistol, played dots, or went bowling?

If you have, then you should already know why it's important to adapt our stance to the target.

Some people can be very accurate but lack of precision, while other can be amazingly precise while inaccurate. And, to score 75% and above at the PMP Exam, we will need both precision and accuracy.

When it comes to firing a gun, before shooting, we must check our anchor points, our posture and stance, and always keep an eye on the target. And if we do everything right, we will score a perfect 10.

Successfully passing on our first try the PMP exam requires the same awareness, philosophy, dedication and continuous hard work. And to adjust our aim, and improve our accuracy and precision at answering the questions of the exam, follow the next steps.

This second phase is composed of 5 activities:
6. Read the PMBOK® Guide
7. Learn the Math's
8. Remember the Project Management Processes
9. Simulate the Exam
10. Don't Forget to Relax

Step #6: Read *PMBOK® Guide* Fifth Edition

The PMP Exam is based on the Project Management Institute® Project Management Body of Knowledge (PMBOK) Guide. Thus, regardless of your current proficiency in the project management discipline, and this sounds silly to say and write, but, I recommend you very strongly to read the *PMBOK® Guide* before considering taking the PMP exam. I also strongly suggest you not to memorize it! Instead, try to understand the inputs, tools and techniques, and outputs of each project management process, and, more importantly, try to implement each process on your own projects.

Indeed, the PMP Exam is not an exam about memorization. It tests our ability to understand and implement the processes. That being said, and assuming you have or will read the *PMBOK® Guide* as part of this essential step in your journey to pass the PMP Certification, the next sections are meant to adjust your aim to successfully pass the PMP Certification: putting an emphasis on critical elements you must understand before sitting in the testing room.

I also want to point out that the points discussed in the next sections are important but, it does not mean that you can overlook the other concepts detailed in the *PMBOK® Guide*. In other words, and as mentioned earlier, we all start our journey from different places, and this means that as you study and prepare yourselves to the PMP Exam, you may find additional key points to capture in your own study notes. So, trust your instinct, and include your findings into your learning objectives and project plan.

But, let's stop the rhetoric here, and start adjusting our aim!

Project Environment

This section is aimed at highlighting the key definitions and information discussed in the first 3 chapters of Project Management Body of Knowledge: Introduction, The Project Management Organizational Influences and Project Lifecycle, and Project Management Processes.

The first 3 chapters provide the background to understand the project environment within the organization culture, style, and business strategy, discussing the organizational process assets and enterprise environmental factors, framing what project governance is, presenting the various project stakeholders, the composition of project team, the role Project Management Office (PMO), etc.

To make a long story short, the next sections highlight what I feel are essential points to understand. But, once again, as you read the *PMBOK® Guide*, create your own study notes, and trust your instinct!

Project vs. Program vs. Portfolio

The *PMBOK® Guide* Fifth Edition defines:

- **Portfolio**: *Projects, programs, sub-portfolios, and operations managed as a group to achieve strategic objectives.*
- **Program**: *A group of related projects, subprograms, and program activities managed in a coordinated way to obtain benefits not available from managing them individually.*
- **Project**: *A temporary endeavor undertaken to create a unique product, service, or result.*

You should know these definitions.

Project Life Cycle vs. Product Life Cycle

A project produces a unique product.

A project has a life cycle, and a product as well.

It is important to understand the differences between the two.

- **Product Life Cycle** is a business technique that attempts to list the stages in the lifespan of commercial/consumer products. Product Life cycle is used for determining the lifespan of these products; such as the normal phases through which a product goes over its lifespan. The typical Product Life Cycle includes 5 stages: Develop, Introduce, Grow, Mature, and Decline.
- **Project Life Cycle** *is the series of phases that a project passes through from its initiation to its closure.* Because projects vary in nature, there is no single defined Life Cycle. Project Life Cycles

range from predictive or plan-driven approaches to adaptive or change-driven approaches.

Project vs. Operations

Projects and Operations have fundamentally different objectives. Projects have a specific objective to attain, while Operations is to sustain the business.

Projects are *temporary endeavors*, operations are ongoing.

Operational tasks produce repetitive outputs.

Projects can intersect with operations during the product life cycle: closeout phase, when developing a new product or enhancing existing functionality, or when retiring a product.

Organizational Structures

Because the organizational structure influences the role and responsibility of project manager, the PMP Exam includes questions focused on the organization structure.

The diagram below shows what is key to remember:

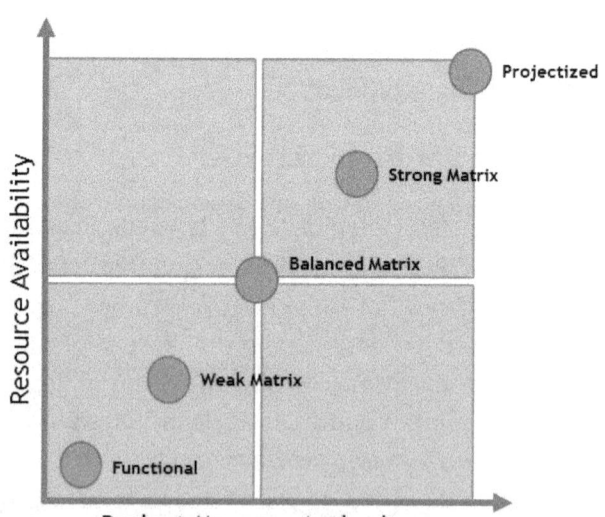

The Five Process Groups

Projects are composed of processes. *A process is set of interrelated actions and activities that are performed to achieve a pre-specified product, service, or result.*

The *PMBOK® Guide* Fifth Edition defines 47 Project Management processes. The processes are concerned with describing and organizing the work of the project.

The Project Management Processes are applicable to most projects, most of the time.

Each process belongs to both a Process Group and a Knowledge Area.

This Process/Process Group/Knowledge Area mapping is critical to understand and remember; we will provide a simple method to easily remember this mapping in *Step #8: Remember the Project Management Processes.* As you read the *PMBOK® Guide*, keep in mind how each process relates to their knowledge area and process group.

As illustrated below, the 5 Process Groups are integrative and iterative.

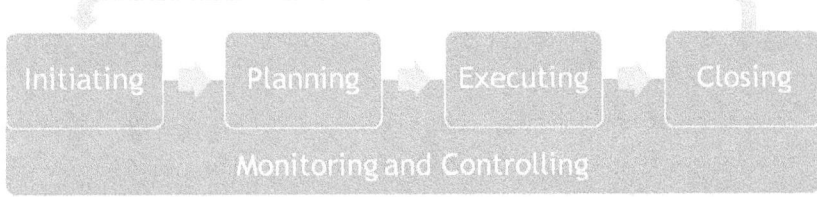

Note: **Process Groups are not the same as Project Phases**; project groups are generally repeated for each phase.

Initiating Process Group

These processes define a new project or a new phase of an existing project by obtaining authorization to start the project or phase. These processes

- Identify the project stakeholders,
- Define the initial scope of work, and
- Commit the initial financial resources required for the project.

The following project management processes belong to the Initiating Process group:

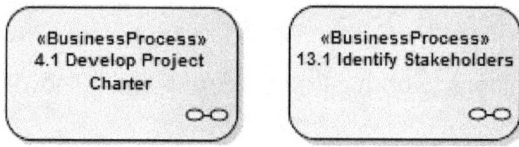

Out of the 200 questions of PMP exam, **13%** focuses on the Initiating Processes.

Planning Process Group

These processes establish the scope of the project, refine the objectives, and define the course of action required to attain the objectives that the project was undertaken to achieve.

The following project management processes belong to the Planning Process group:

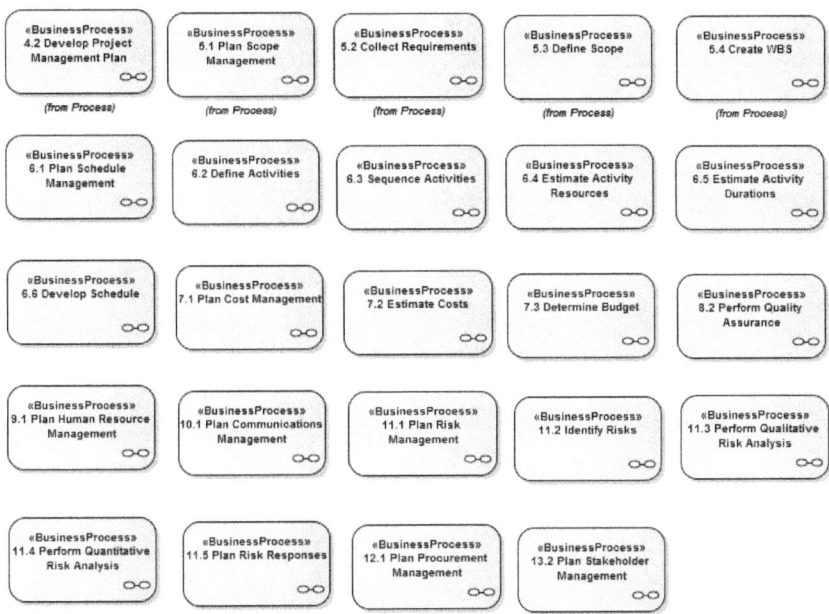

Out of the 200 questions of PMP exam, **24%** focuses on the Planning Processes.

Note: **Planning is an iterative and ongoing process**. This progressive elaboration of project plan is often called *"Rolling Wave Planning."*

Executing Process Group

These processes complete the work defined in the project management plan to satisfy the project specifications. These processes integrate and coordinate people and resources to carry out the work.

The following project management processes belong to the Executing Process group:

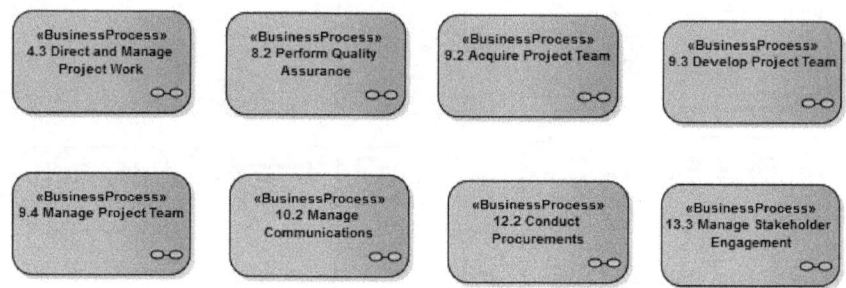

Out of the 200 questions of PMP exam, **30%** focuses on the Executing Processes.

Monitoring & Controlling Process Group

These processes track, review, and regulate the progress and performance of the project; identify any areas in which changes to the plan are required; and initiate the corresponding changes. These processes perform corrective actions as needed and appropriate.

The following project management processes belong to the Monitoring & Controlling Process group:

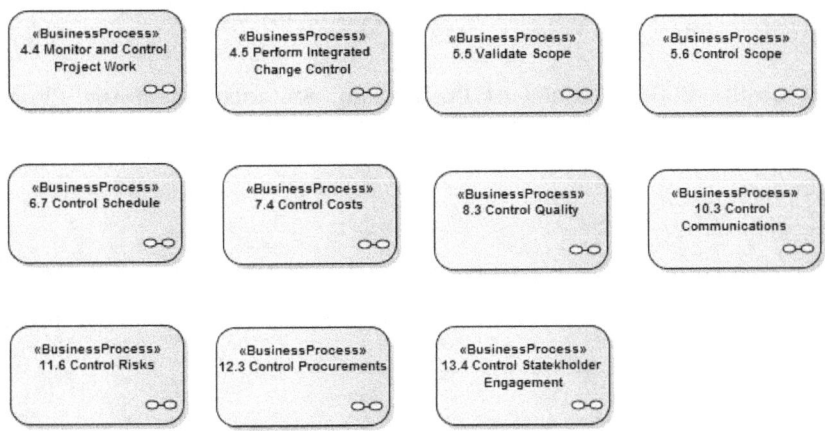

Out of the 200 questions of PMP exam, **25%** focuses on the Monitoring and Controlling Processes.

Closing Process Group

These processes finalize all activities across all Process Groups to formally close the project or phase.

The following processes belong to the Closing Process group:

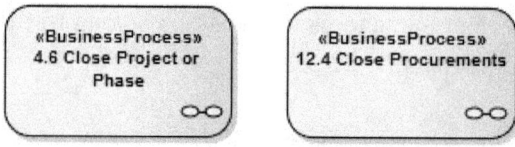

Out of the 200 questions of PMP exam, **8%** focuses on the Closing Processes.

The Ten Knowledge Areas

According to the *PMBOK® Guide*, *"a knowledge area represents a complete set of concepts, terms, and activities that make up a professional field, project management field, or area of specialization."*

Even though you may be an expert in a particular knowledge area, I strongly encourage all candidates to the PMP Exam to spend a minimum of one to three days reading and studying each area. The next 10 sections highlight some of the important concepts and formulas you should master before taking the exam.

Project Integration Management

As you read this chapter in the *PMBOK® Guide*, you must remember that the Project Integration Management processes are integrative processes.

They identify, define, combine, unify, and coordinate the various processes and activities within the Project Management Process Groups.

Project Integration Management involves making trade-offs and decisions based on competitive alternatives, resources availability, and manages the interdependencies between knowledge areas.

The Project Integration Management processes are:

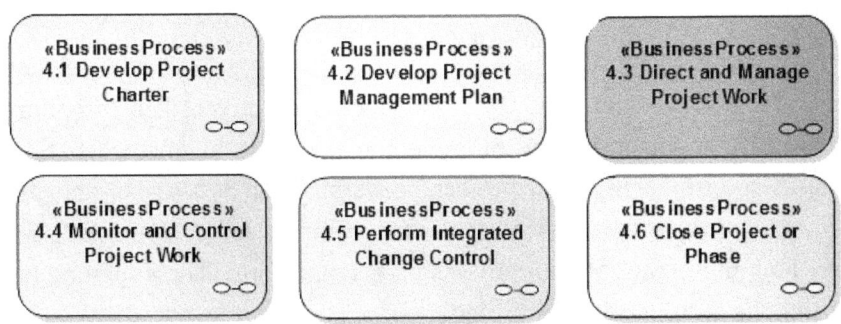

The first Integration process defines the high-level scope of work, developing the foundational document of project: the **Project Charter**. Once approved by the project sponsor, the project is formally authorized.

This provides the assigned project manager with the required authority to acquire resources and initiate the project activities.

Next is to develop a more detailed plan for the project: the **Project Management Plan**. This plan defines how the various project activities are coordinated. This plan integrates all the subsidiary plans that are outputs of the other project management planning processes.

A plan is only a conceptual idea until we actively start executing. Hence, as the project manager, the natural Project Integration Management next process is to Direct and Manage Project Work: to lead and perform the work defined in the plan, and implement any approved changes to the plan.

The integrative nature of these processes imply continuously monitoring and controlling of work being performed. This is done by capturing Work Performance data, transforming the data into Work Performance Information, and offering transparency to all stakeholders by publishing Work Performance Reports.

In this monitoring and controlling activities, the project manager must pay attention to any changes affecting the project goal and implements a well-defined **change control management** to only integrate approved changes into the project scope of work.

At last, as the project continues, and because a project is a temporary endeavor, the responsibility of project manager is to ensure that the project sponsor accepts all project deliverables to finalize all activities across all project processes, thus documenting lessons learned, and enriching the organizational process assets, and formally completing and closing the current phase or project.

Project Scope Management

Project Scope Management processes ensure that the project includes all and only the approved and required work.

As you read this chapter in the *PMBOK® Guide*, do your best in

- Understanding the differences between project and product scope, scope statement and statement of work (SOW),
- Mastering how to develop a Work Breakdown Structure (WBS), and what code of account and control account are.

The Project Scope Management processes are:

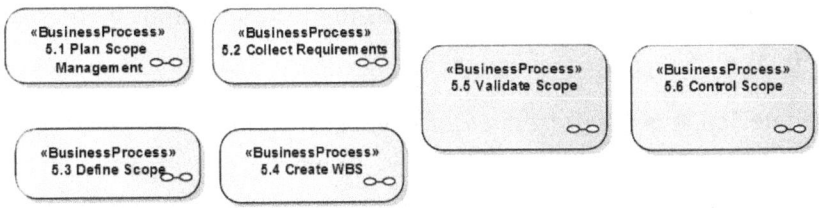

As a project manager, managing the scope is critical for successfully completing your projects. Managing the project scope means to properly plan how the scope will be administered. This is the purpose of Plan Scope Management process where we develop the **Scope Management Plan**.

Knowing how to define the scope of work naturally feeds into the next process: Collect Requirements; You can employ many tools and techniques to gather the requirements for the project, including: benchmarking, context diagrams, document analysis, facilitated workshops, focus groups, group creativity techniques, group decision-making techniques, interviews, observations, prototypes, questionnaires, and surveys. The outputs of this critical process are the requirement documentation and a **Requirement Traceability Matrix**. The documented requirements are then brought forward into the next process: Define Scope.

Defining the scope is to develop a detailed description of the project, and products, services or anticipated results. The primary output of this process is the **Project Scope Statement**; this document includes the project scope description, the project deliverables, the project exclusions, constraints and assumptions. The defined scope must then be organized and subdivided into smaller, more manageable components: this is the objective of the next process: Create WBS.

As you read the *PMBOK® Guide*, pay a close attention to the latter process and the discussed Decomposition technique.

The described processes belong to the Planning process groups. Of course, your work as the project manager does not end with the plan. As the project continues, you must monitor and control that the work being performed by the project team conforms to the defined and agreed scope of work.

Validate Scope is *the process of formalizing acceptance of the completed project deliverables*. This process is primarily concerned with the acceptance of anticipated deliverables.

Control Scope is concerned with monitoring the status of the project and product scope, managing the actual changes when and if the changes occur, and managing changes to the scope baseline. This process must be integrated with the other control processes such as Control Schedule, Control Costs, and Perform Quality Control.

Project Time Management

Managing a project means having a good understanding and control over three pillars: scope, time, and cost. This knowledge area focuses on the second pillar: time.

As you read the relevant chapter in the *PMBOK® Guide*, do your best in comprehending the different types of scheduling charts (GANTT, Milestone, and Networking), the networking methods (Arrow Diagram Method (ADM), Precedence Diagramming Method (PDM), Program Evaluation Review Technique (PERT), and Graphical Evaluation and Review Technique (GERT)), and the concepts of Critical Path and Critical Chain, as well as the various project recovery techniques (crashing, fast-tracking, slack and overtime).

I know it's a lot of things to understand. But, trust me, the PMP Exam will no doubt include questions that are pertinent to these tools, techniques, and concepts.

The Project Time Management processes are:

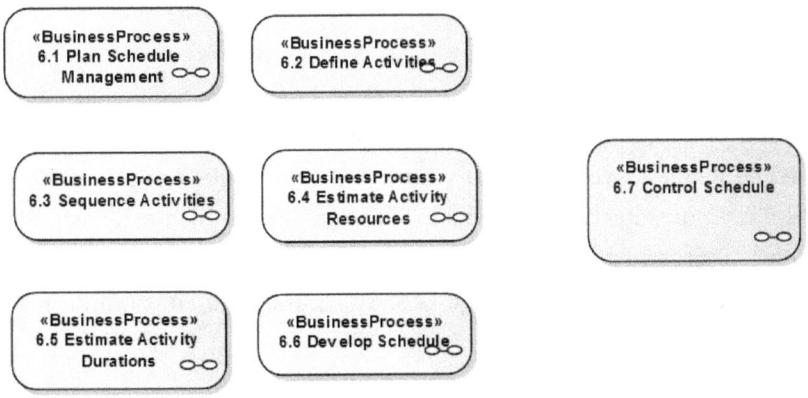

As many other Project Knowledge Areas, the first process consists of *establishing the policies, procedures, and documentation for planning, developing, managing, executing, and controlling the project schedule.* This is the purpose of Plan Schedule Management process.

Once the methodology for managing the schedule is defined, the next step is to define and then sequence the various activities that will develop the project deliverables, and drive the project to its successful completion. Sequencing activities is a critical step in the schedule development effort as it requires a deep understanding of each project activity, and takes into considerations mandatory, discretionary, internal and external dependencies. To sequence the project activities, the project manager leverages various tools and techniques, including: Precedence Diagramming Method, Dependency Determination, Leads and Lags, and Schedule Network Templates.

In most cases, while sequencing the activities, the project manager will work with Subject Matter Experts and leverage the existing organization process assets to estimate the required resources and duration for each activity.

Estimation techniques such as Analogous Estimating, Parametric Estimating, and Three-Point Estimating (including Triangular and Beta distributions) are techniques you should understand before taking the PMP Exam.

After defining, sequencing, and estimating both required resources and duration of project activities, the natural next process is to develop the schedule itself. As you develop your project schedule, keep in mind the logical relationships between tasks (Finish-to-Start, Finish-to-Finish, Start-to-Start, Start-to-Finish, Lead, and Lag), and try understanding how to calculate Early Start, Early Finish, Late Start, and Late Finish, and how to determine each activity's float.

For the PMP Exam, you should be able to calculate the early and late start and finish dates, and the float of each activity on the project schedule. In Step #7: Learn the Math's, I will describe the technique to determine ES, EF, LS, LF and calculate the float of each activity.

The six processes described above all belong to the Planning process group. The remaining Project Time Management process belongs to the

Monitoring and Controlling Process Group: Control Schedule. This process consists of *monitoring the status of project activities to update project progress and manage changes to the schedule baseline to achieve the plan.*

As you read and understand this monitoring and controlling process, focus on comprehending the employed various tools and techniques, and in particular:

- The **Critical Path Method** estimates the minimum project duration and the amount of schedule flexibility (aka total float), and then calculates the early start and finish dates and late start and finish dates of each project activities
- The **Critical Chain Method** modifies the project schedule to account for the available resources, using buffers as appropriate

During the PMP Exam, you may be asked questions pertinent to the Critical Path. So, try to always remember the definition of the Critical Path: *the longest possible continuous pathway taken from the initial event to the terminal event. It determines the total calendar time required for the project; and, therefore, any time delays along the critical path will delay the reaching of the terminal event by at least the same amount.* And, if one question asks you to calculate the free float of critical path, don't waste your time! The float of critical path is per definition: 0! So, keep that in mind.

While you monitor the project schedule, you should as well pay attention on how to calculate the forecast variance of expected duration of a PERT activity, and what Schedule Performance Index (SPI) is and how it is calculated, as well as how to leverage the various scheduling compression techniques and their differences:

- **Crashing** consists in taking action to decrease the total project duration after analyzing a number of alternatives to determine how to get the maximum duration compression for the least cost
- **Fast tracking** is a compression technique consisting in overlapping activities that would normally be done in sequence. This method increases the overall risks on the project.

Project Cost Management

These processes are involved in *planning, estimating, budgeting, financing, funding, managing, and controlling costs so that the project can be completed within the approved budget.*

The concepts behind the Project Cost Management processes are fairly simple to understand. However, this set of processes leverages many calculations that you should be comfortable with, not to say *"know by heart"* and master, before taking the PMP Exam. Most specifically, you should know the terms and calculations associated with Earned Value Analysis, Payback Period, and Return on Investment (ROI), Internal Rate of Return (IRR), Discounted Cash Flow, and Net Present Value (NPV).

The Project Cost Management processes are:

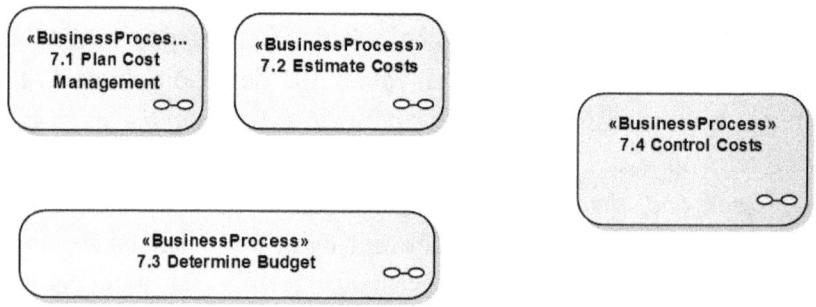

As the project manager, your first task is to establish the policies and procedures for planning, managing and controlling the cost. This first task is the object of Plan Cost Management process during which you develop the **Cost Management Plan**, a component of the Project Management Plan.

The next step is to consider the scope baseline, and the Work Breakdown Structure (WBS) to estimate the costs and then define the budget of project. To do so, you will leverage estimating techniques (e.g.: analogous, bottom-up, three-point, etc.), as well as techniques determining the required financial reserves you will need to properly manage known risks (contingency reserve).

Don't forget that the Management Reserve (i.e.: the reserve allocated to deal with unknown risks) is not part of Project Budget.

The primary output of determining the budget is the **cost baseline**; which is a *time-phased budget used to measure and monitor cost performance,* and usually displayed as an **S-Curve**.

Last but not least, once the project budget is baseline, the project manager must monitor and control the status of project, and update and manage changes to project costs. This is the purpose of the **Control Costs** process.

This monitoring and controlling process relies on the Earned Value Management; a performance measurement technique integrating project scope, cost and schedule (PV, EV, AC, ETC, EAC, CV, SV, CPI, SPI, and TCPI), and making predictions regarding the project's future (i.e.: forecasting).

The next subsection list a few tools and calculations you may want to take a closer look at.

Cost Management Tools

As you prepare for the PMP Exam, and read the *PMBOK® Guide*, it might be interesting to also consider the following additional project cost management tools:

Tools	Description
Benefit Cost Ratio	Benefit Cost Ratio (BCR) measures the expected profitability of a project. • BCR of 1.0 indicates the project is breaking even • BCR of less than 1.0 indicates the project is not financially sound • BCR of more than 1.0 indicates the project is profitable $$Benefit\ Cost\ Ratio = \frac{Present\ Value\ of\ Revenue}{Present\ Value\ of\ Cost}$$

Tools	Description
Depreciation	This refers to two aspects of the same concept: the decrease in value of assets (fair value depreciation), and the allocation of the cost of assets to periods in which the assets are used. Depreciation can be calculated using 2 methods: • Straight-Line Method: take an equal credit during each year • Accelerated Methods: write off the expenses even faster. Accelerated methods include double-declining balance and sum-of-the-years digits.
Future Value	The Future Value indicates how much today's money will grow when compounded at a given rate. $Future\ Value = PV * (1 + i)^n$
Internal Rate of Return (IRR)	IRR is the average rate of return earned over the life of the project. IRR is expressed as a percentage.
Net Present Value	The Net Present Value (NPV) or Net Present Worth (NPW) of a time series of cash flows, both incoming and outgoing, is defined as the sum of the present values (PVs) of the individual cash flows of the same entity. $Net\ Present\ Value = \sum Present\ Value\ of\ Future\ Cash\ F$
Payback Period	This simplistic method calculates the duration to recover the investment by using predicted future cash flows. This method does not take into consideration factors such as inflation, rate of interest, etc. $Payback\ Period = \dfrac{Net\ Investment}{Average\ Annual\ Cash\ Flow}$
Present Value	The Prevent Value is based on the concept that payment received today is worth more than payment received tomorrow. $Present\ Value = \dfrac{Future\ Value}{(1 + i)^n}$

Tools	Description
Return on Investment (ROI)	$$ROI = \dfrac{Net\ Earnings\ After\ Taxes}{Total\ Investment}$$

This knowledge area of Project Management Discipline contains many challenging concepts to understand, and calculations to master.

So, do not hesitate to spend more time on this chapter!

Before taking the PMP Exam, you need to make sure that you know all the tools, techniques and underlying calculations.

But don't worry: You still have time!

I will also get back to these mathematical concepts in our next step: Step #7: Learn the Math's.

Project Quality Management

No luck there! This knowledge area also uses many challenging mathematical tools and techniques you should be comfortable with before taking the PMP Exam. So, be prepared to dive into statistical concepts, quality tools, cost of quality, continuous improvement theories and understand the differences between the Deming, Juran and Crosby quality management approaches. Sounds fun?

More seriously, the *PMBOK® Guide* defines Project Quality Management as *the processes and activities of the performing organization that determine quality policies, objectives, and responsibilities so that the project will satisfy the needs for which it was undertaken.*

That said before discussing the three Project Quality Management processes shown below, let's first emphasize the difference between Quality and Grade:

- **Grade**: *A category or rank used to distinguish items that have the same functional use (e.g., "hammer") but do not share the same requirements for quality (e.g., different hammers may need to withstand different amounts of force)*
- **Quality**: *The degree to which a set of inherent characteristics fulfills requirements*

Low quality is most of the time a problem, low grade may not be.

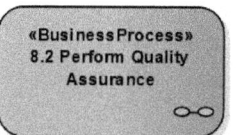

Similar to the other knowledge area, as the project manager, your first task is to define the procedures to manage Quality and deal with Improvements. The Plan Quality Management process generates 4 important outputs: Quality Management Plan, Process Improvement Plan, Quality Metrics and Quality Checklists.

These outputs are then used as inputs to the Perform Quality Assurance and Control Quality processes. Perform Quality Assurance is concerned with making sure that the quality objectives are met, while Control Quality involves monitoring specific project results to determine whether they comply with the relevant quality standards and identifying ways to eliminate the cause of unsatisfactory results.

The 7 Basic Quality Tools

As you plan the approach and procedure to implement quality assurance and perform quality control, seven tools will become handy and helpful to you. As you get familiar with these 7 quality tools, think about their respective application: when to use them, why to them, and what information do they provide you and your team.

Tools	Description
Cause-and-Effect Diagram	Also known as **Fishbone Diagram** or **Ishikawa Diagram**. This is a causal diagram showing the causes of a specific event. It helps the project manager to identify the root cause of a problem and identify a corrective action.
Checksheets	Also known as **Tally sheets**. They are useful to gather data about potential quality problems at the location where the data is generated.
Control Chart	This chart plots the value of a particular variable over time. Control limits are used to identify if the measured process is in or out of control. There are several methods to identify if a process is in control; e.g.: upper/lower limits, and the rule of 7 consecutive points.
Flowchart	Also known as **Process Map**. They are graphical representation of processes, including sequenced activities and decision points.
Histogram	This vertical bar chart shows a graphical representation of the distribution of data. It is an estimate of the probability distribution of a continuous variable.

Tools	Description
Pareto Diagram	Pareto diagram are vertical bar charts with bars ordered by frequency of occurrence. Each bar represents a specific causal category with the height of the bar representing the frequency of the cause. The total of all bars should add up to 100%.
Scatter Diagram	Also known as **Correlation Chart**. This diagram shows the relation of one variable to another variable. The measured/control variable is customarily plotted along the vertical axis.

Quality Concepts

As you read the Project Quality Management knowledge area, remember the difference between Deming's approach to quality, Juran's and Crosby's.

- **William Edwards Deming's** arguments to implement quality is participative, ceasing mass inspection, and improving production and services via education and training. Deming's approach to improvement is a 4-step process: Plan, Do, Check, Act.
- **Joseph Moses Juran**'s approach is based on 3 processes: quality planning, quality control and quality improvement. His philosophy is that the majority of defects are caused by a small percentage of the identifiable problems.
- **Philip Bayard "Phil" Crosby**'s major point is that quality is free, since quality is required to conform to requirements. Quality is prevention, and the performance standard is zero defect.

That being said, regardless if you adopt Crosby's philosophy or not, quality has a cost the project manager must consider in the overall project budget. So, understand the concepts of cost of quality, the cost of conformance, the cost of non-conformance, and the cost of non-quality.

There are also a few concepts to distinguish: Attribute Sampling vs. Variable Sampling, Prevention vs. Inspection, and Special Cause vs. Common Cause, Control Limits vs Tolerances.

It is important as well, especially when controlling quality, to understand how to calculate the standard deviation and the relation with Sigma:

- Two Standard Deviations (+/- 1 Sigma) encompass 68.26% of area
- Four Standard Deviations (+/- 2 Sigma) encompass 95.46% of area
- Six Standard Deviations (+/- 3 Sigma) encompass 99.73% of area
- Twelve Standard Deviations (+/- 6 Sigma) encompass 99.99% of area

At last, let me emphasize the importance of Continuous Improvement Process (CIP) or Kaizen in the Quality Management knowledge area.

- CIP is an ongoing effort to improve products, services, or processes.
- The core principle of CIP is the (self) reflection of processes: Feedback.
- The purpose of CIP is the identification, reduction, and elimination of suboptimal processes: Efficiency.
- The emphasis of CIP is on incremental, continual steps rather than giant leaps: Evolution.

Project Human Resource Management

Project Human Resource Management processes organize, manage, and lead the project team.

The processes are:

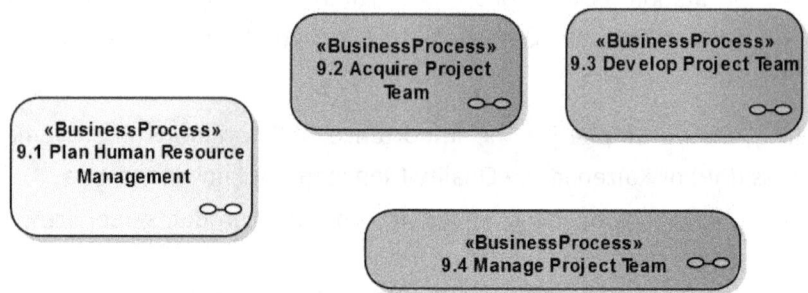

Conceptually, these processes are simple. First, you identify and document project roles, responsibilities, and required skills, and create a staffing plan. You then acquire the staff you need to successfully conduct the project, and develop the acquired team to enhance as appropriate their overall performance (forming, storming, norming, performing, and adjourning). As the project continues, you manage the team, tracking each team member performance, providing feedback as need be (for instance, remember the 360-degree feedback discussed earlier), resolving any potential issues, and submitting any necessary change requests to adjust the team performance.

Behind this apparent simplicity, there are concepts and soft skills that are actually challenging to acquire and understand. Hence, let's take a closer look at these key concepts:

Sources of authority and control

As Project Manager, you will be asked to interact with C-Level executives, upper management, subordinates, functional managers, and people outside your organization. Being able to influence each of these groups is generally important for the success of your projects.

Based on your experience, you will source your authority and control from various sources:
1. Bureaucratic
2. Charismatic/Persuasive
3. Coercive
4. Expert
5. Formal
6. Referent
7. Resource Control
8. Reward

Various leadership styles

The situational leadership theory is a theory first introduced as "*Life Cycle Theory of Leadership*". The fundamental underpinning of the situational leadership theory is that there is no single "*best*" style of leadership. Effective leadership is task-relevant, and the most successful leaders are those that adapt their leadership style to the maturity of the individual or group they are attempting to lead or influence. Effective leadership varies, not only with the person or group that is being influenced, but it also depends on the task, job or function that needs to be accomplished.

As a project manager, you need to be aware of your natural leadership style and adapt it to the current situation. There are several leadership styles:
1. Autocratic / Directive
2. Consensus Manager / Participating
3. Consultative Autocrat / Persuading
4. Delegating
5. Shareholder Manager (also considered as poor management)

Different motivation theories of human behavior

Be warned: the PMP Exam loves these motivation theories! Here are the most common ones:
1. Maslow's Hierarchy of Needs: Physiology > Security > Social > Self-Esteem > Self-Actualization

2. Hertzberg's Theory of Motivation: Hygiene Factors (pay, working conditions) destroy motivation, while Motivators (opportunity to achieve self-actualization) improve motivation
3. McGregor's Theory X: People dislike their work and will do everything they can to avoid it
4. McGregor's Theory Y: People are high performer, creative, committed and self-discipline
5. Ouchi's Theory Z: Management deems workers as trustworthy and capable

Methods of managing conflicts

There are five methods to manage and resolve conflicts:

- Withdraw / Avoid: Retreat from actual or potential conflicting situations; this is a Lose-Lose
- Smooth / Accommodate: Emphasize commonalities; this is also a Lose-Lose approach
- Compromise / Bargain / Reconcile: Give up something for finding a common ground between parties; this is a Lose-Lose.
- Force / Direct / Coerce : Exert one's view at the expense of the others; this is a Win-Lose
- Collaborate / Problem Solve: Address directly the root of disagreements; the conflict is treated as a problem. This is a Win-Win.

Techniques to team building

Team building is a philosophy of job design in which employees are viewed as members of interdependent teams instead of as individual workers. The purpose of Team Building is to get each team member to focus on the big-picture and to concentrate on the project goal.

Team building refers to a wide range of activities designed for improving team performance.

Project Communications Management

Similar to the Human Resource Management knowledge area, Communications Management is a simple knowledge area from a process standpoint since it only contains three processes shown below.

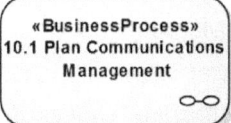

You first plan how/when you will communicate to your various stakeholders. You then manage the communications, ensuring transparent and frequent information distribution, and as the project continues, you naturally monitor and control the status of your communications, addressing any concerns before they become issues or risks, and submitting any required change requests.

In English, these processes are simple to understand. However, there are a few concepts and one formula to master when preparing for the PMP Exam.

As you read the *PMBOK® Guide*, pay a close attention to the following concepts:

Active and Effective Listening

Active Listening requires patience, self-control, empathy, and a willingness to understand the other's point of view.

Effective Listening is the ability to recognize the importance of verbal and nonverbal listening behaviors, including body language, and the ability to utilize gestures and body language consciously.

Remember this formula from Albert Meharabian about the importance of nonverbal communication:

> Total Message Impact = Words (7%) + Vocal Tones (38%) + Facial Expressions (55%)

Communication Barriers

Communication Barriers are obstacles to the communications such as: distance, noise, cultural differences, limited or withholding information, terminology, hidden agenda, etc.

Communication Model and Channels

Understanding the Sender-Receive Communication Model belongs to the General Management skillsets. The basic communication model can be summarized by the following flow: Encode > Transmit > Decode > Acknowledge > Feedback/Response.

The number of communication channels is calculated by the following formula, where n is the number of stakeholders:

$$Channels = n * \frac{(n-1)}{2}$$

The PMP Exam will likely include a question requiring you to calculate the number of communication channels.

Keep in mind as well the three basic communication channels:
1. Upward Communication (vertically or diagonally)
2. Downward Communication (vertically or diagonally)
3. Lateral Communication (horizontally)

Four Major Communication Styles

As a project manager, you will spend 75% to 90% of your time communicating! Adapting your communication style will be key to convey your message, motivate your team, and resolve problems. To be an effective communicator, you have to adapt your communication style to your interlocutor's personality:
1. Abstract-Random: The Intuitive Free Thinker
2. Abstract-Sequential: The Organizer
3. Concrete-Random: The Explorer / Entrepreneur
4. Concrete-Sequential: The Fixer

Project Risk Management

According to the *PMBOK® Guide, Project Risk Management includes the processes of conducting risk management planning, identification, analysis, response planning, and controlling risk on a project.*

When studying this critical knowledge area of the project management discipline, you should focus on:

- Understanding the inputs, tools and techniques, and outputs of each process
- Appreciating the various techniques to identify risks and opportunities; including but not limited to: Brainstorming, Delphi technique, interviewing, SWOT, and assumption analysis
- Recognizing the relationship of risk and project life cycle: The probability of successfully completing the project is lowest at the start. Hence, risks are highest at the start of project
- Realizing that risks can have a negative or positive impacts on the project
- Classifying risks: business, pure, known and unknown
- Understanding the different risk assessment analysis techniques; e.g.: Decision Tree, Expected Monetary Value, Monte Carlo Analysis, Ishikawa diagram
- Determining the value of a risk event: $R = P * I$; where P is the probability of the occurrence, and I the impact of the risk should it occur
- Developing appropriate mitigation and risks responses

The Project Risk Management processes are:

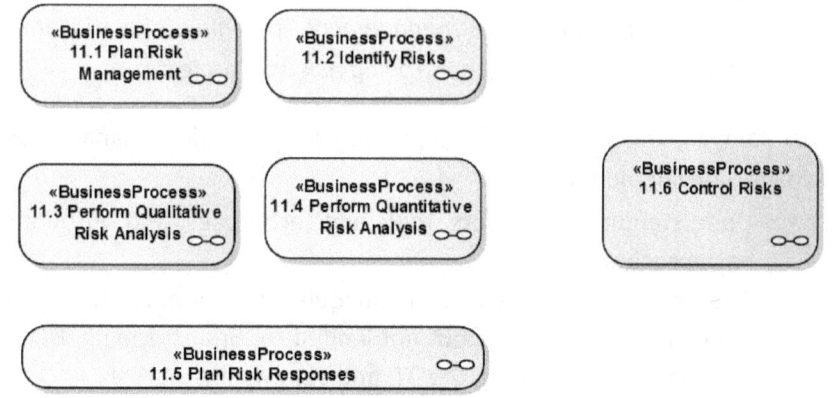

Qualitative vs. Quantitative Risk Analysis

Qualitative risk analysis aims at prioritizing the identified risks using a rating scale. Risks are scored based on their likelihood of occurrence and the impact on project objectives should they occur.

Quantitative risk analysis is generally performed for the highest priority risks. Quantitative risk analysis determines numerical rating for these risks.

Probability determination is important in quantitative risk analysis, but don't worry, we will cover the simple probability concepts in Step #7: Learn the Math's!

Strategies to manage Risks

Negative Risks or Threats	Positive Risks or Opportunities
• **Avoid**: Change the Project Plan to eliminate the risk • **Transfer**: Shift the consequence to a third-party or purchase an insurance • **Mitigate**: Reduce the probability of impact and adverse risk event to an acceptable level • **Accept**: Make a conscious decision not to change and do anything	• **Exploit**: Change the Project Plan to ensure the opportunity occurs • **Share**: Assign ownership to a third-party • **Enhance**: Increase probability of opportunity to occur • **Accept**: Make a conscious decision not to change and do anything

Project Procurement Management

Procurement Management involves the end-to-end business processes of selling that are responsible for managing prospective sellers, qualification and education of the seller and to the matching of seller's expectations to the project objectives and the ability of sellers to deliver the anticipated deliverables. Hence, these processes are responsible for managing response to RFI and RFP. In short, this knowledge area of the project management discipline requires a wide-range of competencies.

But, let's not get ahead of ourselves, and focus simply on the Procurement Management processes as defined in the Guide to Project Management Body of Knowledge, Fifth Edition:

 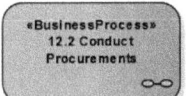  

One important note as you read these processes is to understand the point of view of *PMBOK® Guide* in the seller-buyer relationship: the Project Procurement Management processes are discussed from the buyer perspective; nonetheless, remember that project management is done by both buyer and seller.

As you get familiar with this knowledge area, other key elements to study and understand are:

Contract types

As you plan how you will be conducting procurements and controlling your seller performance, a key question that will rapidly surface is the type of contract you should use. Contracts generally fall under 3 categories:

1) Fixed-Price,
2) Cost-Reimbursable, and
3) Time and Material (T&M).

Depending on your organization risk acceptance level, you may want to consider different contract types. The below diagram shows where the risk primarily lays for each contract type:

- FFP : Firm-Fixed-Price, also called Lump-Sum
- FPI : Fixed Price-Plus-Incentive-Fee
- T&M : Time & Material
- CPIF : Cost-Plus-Incentive-Fee
- CPAF : Cost-Plus-Award-Fee
- CPFF : Cost-Plus-Fixed-Fee
- CPPC : Cost-Plus-a-Percentage of Cost

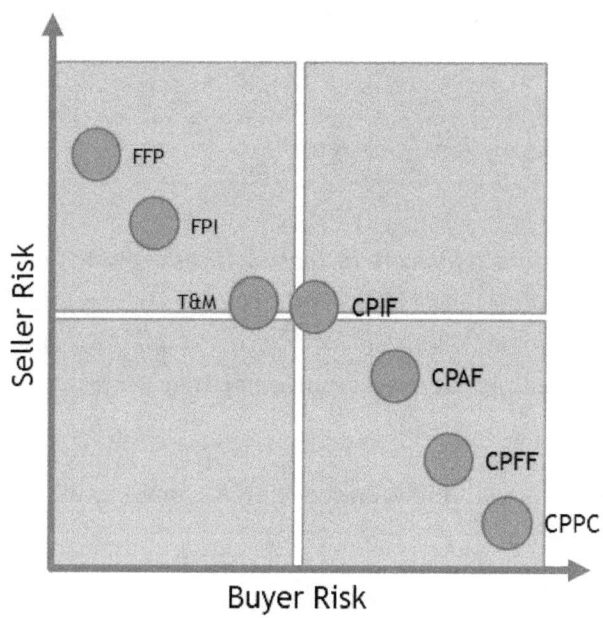

As you start the contract negotiations, keep in mind the basic ground rules:

- The seller wants to maximize the profit potential while minimizing risks
- The buyer wants to maintain an incentive for efficient and economical performance while placing maximum risk on the seller
- The buyer must inform potential sellers of any known risks on the procurement scope of work

The *PMBOK® Guide* may not discuss in much details the stages and tactics of contract negotiation, however the PMP Exam will most certainly ask you practical questions about the procurement processes and use terms relevant to the negotiation stages and tactics. Hence, the Project Manager should be familiar with the following stages:

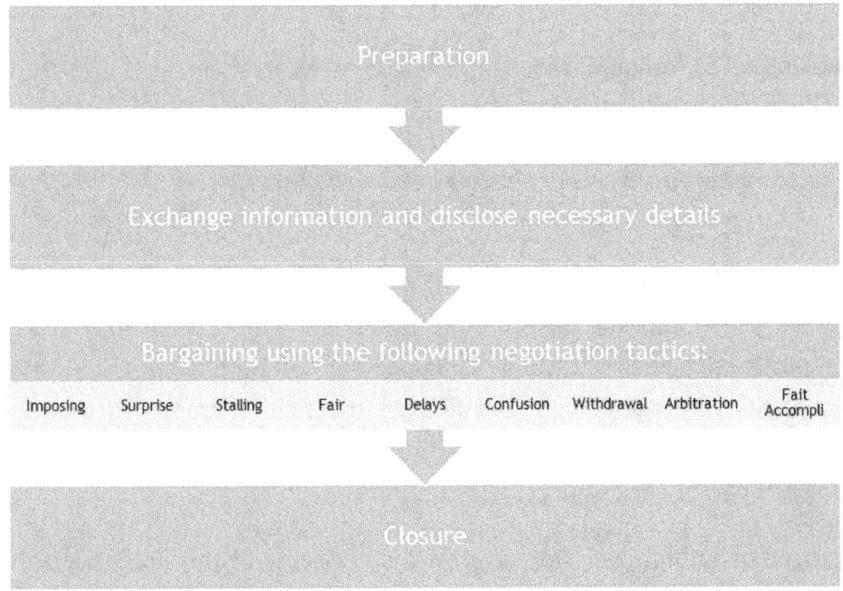

Project Stakeholder Management

The last knowledge area discussed in the *PMBOK® Guide* is the Project Stakeholder Management, which *includes the processes required to identify the people, groups, or organizations that could impact or be impacted by the project, to analyze stakeholder expectations and their impact on the project, and to develop appropriate management strategies for effectively engaging stakeholders in project decisions and execution*

The Project Stakeholder Management processes are:

 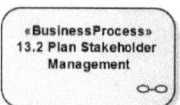  

One of the first processes the project manager must perform is to identify the people, groups and organizations that could impact or be impacted by the project activities or results. An important notion to understand is that the ability of stakeholders to influence the final characteristics of the project product is highest at the start of the project, and becomes progressively lower as the project continues.

This puts an additional emphasis on the criticality of this process on the outcome of project: without the right stakeholders and without their respective required level of engagement, collecting requirements, defining the scope, approving change requests, validating the developed products, services or results will be if not impossible, extremely challenging – not to say *'meaningless.'*

As you identify your project stakeholders, classify them using a model such as the Power/Interest grid, the Power/Influence grid, the Influence/Impact grid, or the Salience Model.

Once identified and classified, the next step is to define the level of engagement you expect for the project to be successful. Managing and Controlling Stakeholder engagement means that you can measure their level of engagement.

The *PMBOK® Guide* refers to the below scale:

- Unware: the stakeholder is unaware of project, project goal, and potential impacts
- Resistant: the stakeholder is aware of project and is resistant to the targeted change
- Neutral: the stakeholder knows of project but is yet neither supportive or resistant
- Supportive: the stakeholder knows of project existence and goal and supports the change
- Leading: the stakeholder is aware of project and potential impacts, and is actively engaged in the project, and pushes for the project to be completed successfully

This scale is used to develop the **Stakeholder Engagement Assessment Matrix**.

Throughout the project, from initiation to closure, the project must ensure a clear, transparent and adequate information distribution to the various stakeholders.

Having classified and defined the expected level of engagement for each stakeholder also provides a key input for the project manager's strategy to:

- Increase support and reduce resistance of stakeholders
- Identify and address actively concerns before they become issues or risks
- Drive adoption of project goal and potential impacts
- Maintain or increase the efficiency and effectiveness of stakeholder engagement.

This is it!

Congratulations on reading the main sections of *PMBOK® Guide*!

But, as time allows, I still recommend you to read the different appendices, especially the one describing the interpersonal skillsets. The PMP Exam includes questions pertinent to the soft skills of project management discipline.

Step #7: Learn the Math's!

Probability, Graph Theory, Algebra; let's face it and be prepared: The PMP Exam does include questions where mastering mathematics is unavoidable to correctly answer.

If this sounds scary, don't worry!

Hereafter are one-pagers with key formulas you need to know in order to answer with flying colors these apparently challenging questions.

Applied Mathematics to Time Management

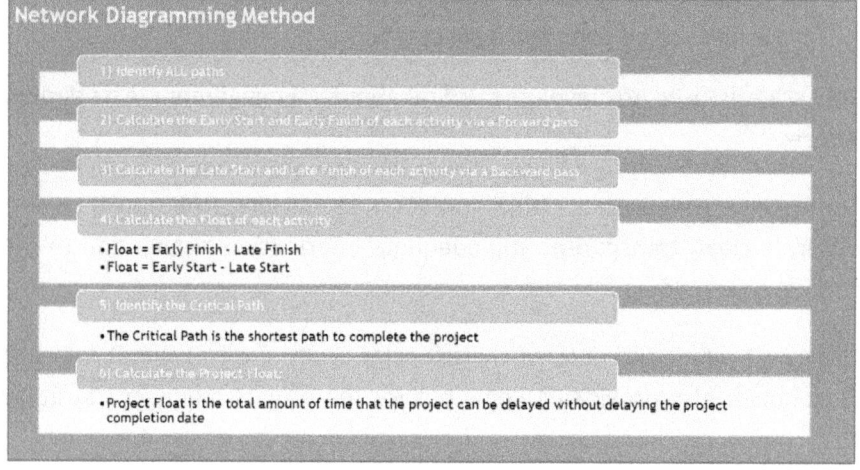

Network Diagramming Method

1) Identify ALL paths

2) Calculate the Early Start and Early Finish of each activity via a Forward pass

3) Calculate the Late Start and Late Finish of each activity via a Backward pass

4) Calculate the Float of each activity
  • Float = Early Finish - Late Finish
  • Float = Early Start - Late Start

5) Identify the Critical Path
  • The Critical Path is the shortest path to complete the project

6) Calculate the Project Float:
  • Project Float is the total amount of time that the project can be delayed without delaying the project completion date

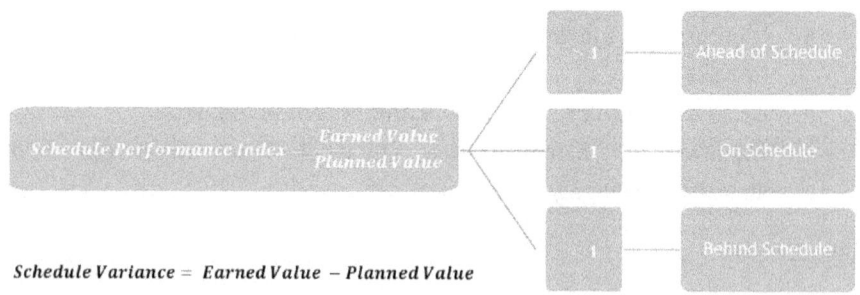

Schedule Performance Index $= \dfrac{Earned\ Value}{Planned\ Value}$

> 1	Ahead of Schedule
1	On Schedule
< 1	Behind Schedule

$Schedule\ Variance = Earned\ Value - Planned\ Value$

Applied Mathematics to Cost Management

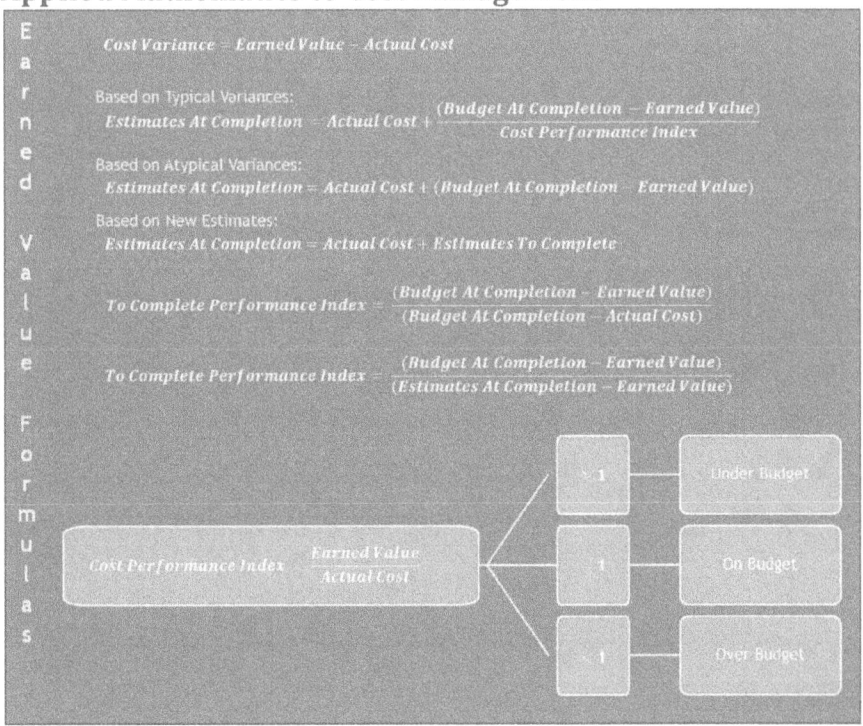

$$Cost\ Variance = Earned\ Value - Actual\ Cost$$

Based on Typical Variances:
$$Estimates\ At\ Completion = Actual\ Cost + \frac{(Budget\ At\ Completion - Earned\ Value)}{Cost\ Performance\ Index}$$

Based on Atypical Variances:
$$Estimates\ At\ Completion = Actual\ Cost + (Budget\ At\ Completion - Earned\ Value)$$

Based on New Estimates:
$$Estimates\ At\ Completion = Actual\ Cost + Estimates\ To\ Complete$$

$$To\ Complete\ Performance\ Index = \frac{(Budget\ At\ Completion - Earned\ Value)}{(Budget\ At\ Completion - Actual\ Cost)}$$

$$To\ Complete\ Performance\ Index = \frac{(Budget\ At\ Completion - Earned\ Value)}{(Estimates\ At\ Completion - Earned\ Value)}$$

$$Cost\ Performance\ Index = \frac{Earned\ Value}{Actual\ Cost}$$

> 1 — Under Budget

1 — On Budget

< 1 — Over Budget

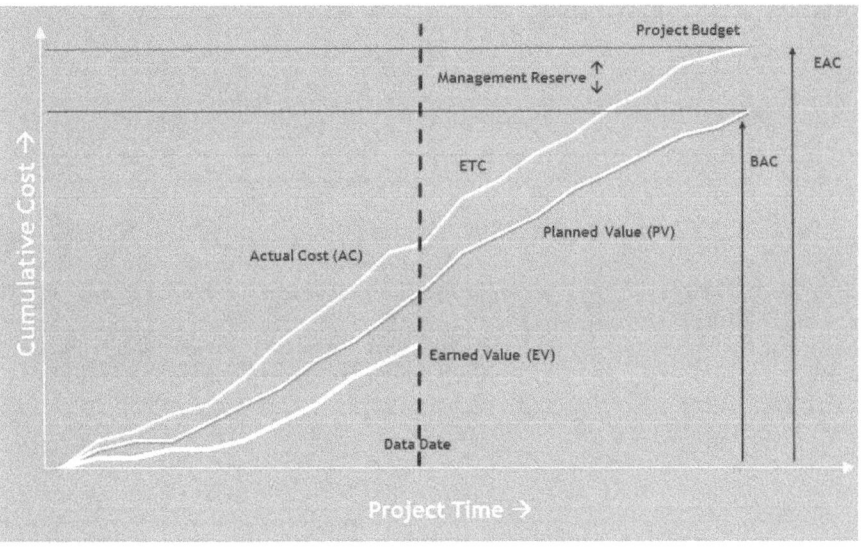

Reliability of Cost Estimates

Cost Estimate: -10% to +15%
Definitive Estimate: -15% to +20%
Preliminary Estimate: -20% to +30%
Conceptual Estimate: -30% to +50%
Order of Magnitude Estimate: -50% to +50%

Three Data Points Estimates

Most Likely: TM
Optimistic: TO
Pessimistic: TP

$$Mean\ Estimate, TE = \frac{TO + 4\,TM + TP}{6}$$

$$Standard\ Deviation\ of\ the\ Estimate = \frac{TP - TO}{6}$$

Depreciation

$$Sum\ of\ the\ Years\ Depreciation = Depreciable\ Base \times \frac{Remaing\ Useful\ Life}{Sum\ of\ the\ Years'\ Digits}$$

$$Depreciable\ Base = Original\ Cost - Salavage\ Value$$

$$Sum\ of\ the\ Year's\ Digits = \frac{n(n+1)}{2}$$ Where n is the useful life of the asset in years

Applied Mathematics to Quality Management

Control Chart

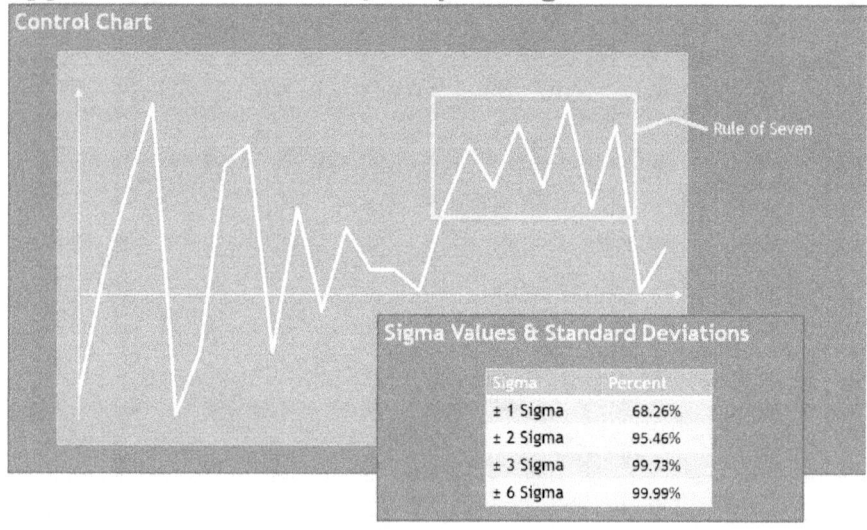

Rule of Seven

Sigma Values & Standard Deviations

Sigma	Percent
± 1 Sigma	68.26%
± 2 Sigma	95.46%
± 3 Sigma	99.73%
± 6 Sigma	99.99%

Applied Mathematics to Risk Management

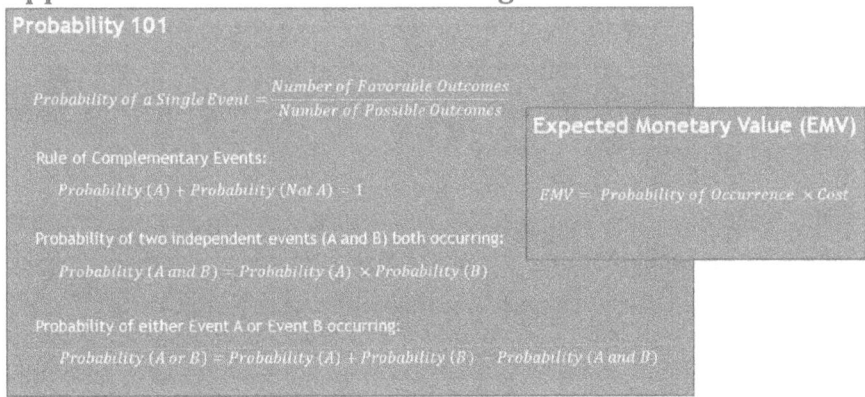

FREE GIFT: The One-Pager Formula

To thank you for purchasing this book, I have embedded into The 3-by-5 Steps Accelerators a One-Pager Formula for you to print and use as you work on your PMP.

I hope this one-pager will be of any help!

The 3-by-5 Steps Accelerator is available to download at:

http://www.advencys.com/the3by5freebonus.html

Step #8: Remember the Project Management Processes

The *PMBOK® Guide* Fifth Edition introduces 5 new processes; 5 additional processes to learn, and understand in and out; 5 new challenges to take up, but, trust me, learning 5 new processes is easy compared to practicing and then mastering them.

In this section, I am going to summarize one of the most efficient techniques to remember in 5 minutes or less, not only these 5 new processes, but all the 47 Project Management processes!

When you are about to take the PMP Exam, go for an interview, or simply explain to a coworker the Project Management Processes, being able to quickly, accurately and precisely describe the 47 processes on a one-pager is a key differentiator between a project manager and a certified project manager.

Remember the Process Groups numbers!

So, let's start by the numbers:

- 47 Project Management processes spread among
- 5 process groups, and
- 10 knowledge areas:

Initiating	Planning	Executing	Monitoring & Controlling	Closing
2	24	8	11	2

Next, remember the numbering of each knowledge area:

4. Integration
5. Scope
6. Time
7. Cost
8. Quality
9. Human Resource
10. Communication
11. Risk
12. Procurement
13. Stakeholder

Then, think about the Initiating & Closing process groups; they are the easiest ones, since both have only 2 processes:

Initiating	Closing
4.1: Develop Project Charter	4.6: Close Project or Phase
13.1: Identify Stakeholder	12.4: Close Procurement

This leaves us with 43 processes and 3 Process Groups to focus on. 43 processes may sound like a lot to memorize but, you don't have to! You simply have to memorize 9 processes, and remember 7 words:
- Plan,
- Estimate,
- Perform,
- Develop,
- Control,
- Manage, and
- Validate.

Ten *Plan* processes – which belong to the Planning Process Group
- 5.1: Plan Scope Management
- 6.1: Plan Schedule Management
- 7.1: Plan Cost Management
- 8.1: Plan Quality Management
- 9.1: Plan Human Resource Management
- 10.1: Plan Communication Management
- 11.1: Plan Risk Management
- 11.5: Plan Risk Responses
- 12.1: Plan Procurement
- 13.2: Plan Stakeholder Management

During the PMP exam, if there is any question stating a "*plan*" process, you should know that you are in the Planning phase of the project.

Three *Estimate* processes – which belong to the Planning Process Group
- 6.4: Estimate Activity Resources
- 6.5: Estimate Activity Duration
- 7.2: Estimate Costs

Four *Perform* processes
- 4.5: Perform Integrated Change Control
- 8.2: Perform Quality Assurance
- 11.3: Perform Qualitative Risk Analysis
- 11.4: Perform Quantitative Risk Analysis

The first one belongs to Monitoring & Controlling Process Group (it includes the *"Control"* word). *"Perform Quality Assurance"* processes belong to the Executing Process Group, and the last two belong to the Planning Process Group.

Three *Develop* processes
- 4.2: Develop Project Management Plan
- 6.6: Develop Schedule
- 9.3: Develop Project Team

The *"Develop Project Team"* belongs to the Executing Process Group, and the two first processes to the Planning Process Group.

Nine *Control* processes – which belong to the Monitoring & Controlling Process Group
- 4.4: Monitor & Control Project Work
- 5.6: Control Scope
- 6.7: Control Schedule
- 7.4: Control Costs
- 8.3: Control Quality
- 10.3: Control Communications
- 11.6: Control Risks
- 12.3: Control Procurements
- 13.4: Control Stakeholder Engagement

Four *Manage* processes – which belong to the Executing
Process Group
- 4.3: Direct and Manage Project Work
- 9.4: Manage Project Team
- 10.2: Manage Communications
- 13.3: Manage Stakeholder Engagement

One *Validate* process – which belongs to the Monitoring &
Controlling Process Group
- 5.5: Validate Scope

What's left to memorize? Nine Processes

Planning	Executing
5.2: Collect Requirements	9.2: Acquire Project Team
5.3: Define Scope	12.2: Conduct Procurements
5.4: Create WBS	
6.2: Define Activities	
6.3: Sequence Activities	
7.3: Determine Budget	
11.2: Identify Risks	

Step #9: Simulate the Exam

Congratulations; you are almost there! But, are you ready to tackle this next step?

This next step is meant to complete the study phase of your personal and professional improvement initiative, aiming at successfully taking the PMP exam.

On one hand, reading, understanding and practicing the project management processes, comprehending and mastering the applied mathematics of this particular and always evolving discipline, are the foundational blocks you need to pass the PMP Certification.

On the other hand, you must remember your parents, coaches, or teachers telling you a thousand time the old adage: *"practice makes perfect."* Regardless of your feelings about this proverb, one thing is clear: training always improves performance.

In our earlier project plan, we set aside about 10 days to solely focus on simulating the exam. Many candidates to the PMP Certification find it very useful to take a few exam simulations toward the end of their preparation. Simulating the PMP Exam is indeed the most direct and efficient way to determine if you are indeed ready for the exam or if you should postpone the date.

So, consider simulating the PMP exam at least two weeks before D Day.

And if I may, let me add that you might want to introduce simulations earlier in your project plan, and actually, throughout your studies. This will provide you constant feedback on the progress you made.

Now, the question you can ask yourself is how to best simulate the PMP Exam?

Good question!

On the positive side, there are many books offering practice questions, including my most recent work for project managers:

Practice and Pass the PMP® Exam

There are also websites provide a 90-day subscription access to an actual PMP Exam simulator. However, they generally require a subscription fee, going from US $59 up to US $129:

- http://www.pmtraining.com: US $59 for accessing to 1000+ questions
- http://www.pm-exam-simulator.com: US $99 for accessing to 1,800 questions
- http://www.pmfinal.com: US $129 for accessing to 1000+ questions

At last, you have software-based PMP Exam Simulators, including the best-selling Rita Mulcahy's PM FASTrack simulator and the *"PMP Exam Simulation Software"* developed by 4 certified project managers and offering more than 6000 questions. However, these solutions are either expensive or not based on the latest edition of PMBOK® Guide.

You can also check the new **Master the Project Management Discipline** Product Suite developed by ADVENCYS (http://advencys.com), a small company based in Seattle, Washington.

Their product offerings include a PMP Exam Simulator. But, to be completely transparent with you, I must tell you that I work on this product.

So, I may not be the best person to provide you any objective recommendations, but I still invite you to check their **PMP Exam Simulator Professional Edition**.

That said, and marketing aside, I strongly recommend continually taking different quizzes and mock exams throughout your journey, and especially when you are deeply engaged in reading the *PMBOK® Guide*. It will help you in becoming familiar with not only the processes and formulas of project management discipline, but as well give you confidence about your learnings.

How do you know if you can feel confident about the real exam? By consistently scoring above 75%...

Naturally to score above 75%, you must have a good comprehension of *PMBOK® Guide*, and understand the PMI's viewpoint on each process. More importantly, you must have a strategy!

So, let me give you a few important tips about the PMP Exam:
1. Before starting the exam, do a brain dump! In Step #11, I will discuss this exercise in details
2. The *PMBOK® Guide* is the reference for all correct answers
3. Be aware of time, and don't spend too much time on one question! you have 200 questions to answer in 4 hours; this means, you have a little more than 1 minute per question
4. Pace yourself! Taking a 4-hour exam can be intense and stressful. Leverage the first 3 hours to go through as many questions as you can (if not all), and during the last hour, go back the questions you were unsure or did not respond to
5. Take your time reading carefully the question, especially if this is a scenario question
6. Many questions are designed to be long and made to confuse you, So always ask yourself what the real question is, and most of the time, the last sentence includes the real question
7. Don't read more into a question; there is no trick
8. When you are not sure about an answer, first eliminate the obviously wrong answers, and pick one; if you can eliminate 2 answers, you have increase your chance by 50%
9. Don't leave any questions unanswered! Leaving a question blank always leads to 0. Hence, even if you don't know, just guess; you still have 25% of chance to answer correctly
10. Do the simple math in your head, but if you are uncertain, do the calculations on paper!

At last, as you practice and simulate the PMP Exam, you should track your score and confidence level answering particular questions:

- Are questions relevant to a particular knowledge area becoming easier to answer properly?
- Do you feel more confident about questions requiring mastering applied mathematics?

Ask yourself those sorts of question, and answer them objectively will drastically help you adjust your focus on the specific areas you need additional tune-up.

Remember what we discussed earlier:

- Everything we do in life can be considered as a project
- Project Planning is an iterative and ongoing process

What does it mean? It means that even though we spent time planning this journey, our path to the PMP Certification is and will not be a simple straight-line to follow. As any other projects, changes happen and we must adapt and integrate these changes into our plan.

Thus, as you learn more about the inputs, tools and techniques, and outputs of project management processes, and better understand your strengths and weaknesses, don't be afraid of changing your strategy to increase your opportunities at passing the PMP Certification.

Step #10: Don't Forget to Relax

Allow me to take a guess: studying for the PMP exam is not your fulltime job.

Hence when you decided to begin this journey, you had accepted to set aside part of your personal time to complete this journey. Instead of playing with your kids, attending one of their recitals, going on a date with your significant other, visiting your parents, taking a road trip on the Louisiana's Highway 31, vacationing on the Big Island, or hiking through the rainforests along the Cascade Loop, you have committed your past evenings and weekends to study in a coffee shop, in your office or at home.

Taking the PMP Exam is a high-stress event, and studying hard is your best and sole alternative to succeed. Thus far, and be honest with yourself, you have done everything right:

1. You set your learning objectives
2. You planned your journey
3. You applied and qualified for the PMP Certification
4. You scheduled your PMP Exam
5. You read the *PMBOK® Guide*
6. You learned the applied mathematics to the project management discipline
7. You understood and can draft on paper the relationships between process groups, knowledge areas and project management processes
8. You completed many quizzes and simulated several PMP Exams

On the other hand, have you forgotten the name of this second phase?

Study with Intelligence.

You are working fulltime and have spent almost 7 weeks studying hard to slowly get ready for D Day.

Now, before closing this second phase, and opening the curtain on the third and final phase, remember to relax!

Relax, and take a short break!

As a project manager, soon to be certified, you must recognize the value and importance to celebrate a key milestone with your project team.

After all, even though you are the one who did all this work, you are most likely not the only one who sacrificed a lot in this journey. Think about your family, friends or coworkers who continuously supported you in this endeavor. They shared their own personal experience preparing for the PMP Exam. They brought you a cup of coffee when you were tired. They did not cry when you could not attend their baseball game. They avoided disturbing you when you were so focused on reading your training materials. They were here, present, and always supportive throughout your journey.

So, today, close your training materials, stop this PMP Exam Simulator, put on the side your study notes, turn-off your computer, and enjoy relaxing with your family and friends!

3   Get Ready for D Day

I know! I was not supposed to tell you more about my childhood growing up in Italy, and going on our yearly family vacation. So, I guess, I lied, or should I say, I decided to approve and implement one of this last minute change request into my own writing journey.

Hence, as I was explaining earlier, two weeks prior to our departure, my parents held a family meeting to share with us their plan, our upcoming destination, and set the plan in motion. The next 2 weeks were generally passing by very fast. My older brother and I were focused on taking care of the chores my parents gave us to complete.

One year, because my brother came down with a bad cold, my mom decided to reassign some of his tasks to me. Not only did I have to pack all the things I wanted to take for our vacation, I had to assist my brother packing his own stuff. And, as if I did not have anything else to do, the weekend before leaving, my Dad asked me to help him in cleaning the garage.

I was overwhelmed, and clearly angry.

I felt as if I had no control on anything.

I felt I was rushing to complete everything I had on my to-do list before going on vacation.

As you can guess, on the morning of our departure, I had barely the time to complete packing my stuff and my brother's. And, the garage was... well... not much cleaner than a few days before.

Of course, being 11 years old, I was certain my parents were going to punish me for not having completing all the chores they wanted me to do. But, nothing happened!

We all took place in my parents' old Fiat, my brother who was feeling better, sitting next to me, and just like that, we were on our way to Aosta.

Looking back, and thinking as a project manager, instead of rushing and doing a half-done job, I should have told my Dad that I was unable to complete my task on time. Informed of my setback, my Dad could have then decided to postpone our departure if he wanted the garage to be spotless before we leave.

We did however left, and never talked about the garage. Hence, I assumed, my dad's asking was only to keep me busy and away from my older brother; My Dad basically wanted me to leave my brother alone, and allow him to rest and sufficiently recover from his cold. My Dad was amazingly smart!

That said, as you look back at your own journey, and look forward to your upcoming exam, your D Day, my questions to you are simple:
- Do you feel overwhelmed?
- Do you feel you are rushing your studies?

If so, you may want to consider postponing your PMP Exam. Rescheduling the exam within 30 calendar days of the D Day comes with a US $70 fee, but trust me, it's cheaper to reschedule than to fail.

Why am I asking such questions? Why am I even suggesting you to postpone your exam? Because you must feel as prepared as you can be, before moving forward with the next steps.

This third and final phase is divided into the 5 following steps:
11. Train for a 5-Minute Brain Dump
12. Prepare the Final Logistics
13. Stop Studying and Sleep Well
14. Start your Exam with Confidence
15. Join the PMI Community

So, let's get ready!

Step #11: Train for a 5-Minute Brain Dump

At the testing center, after logging onto your session, and before starting the exam, you will be invited to watch a tutorial to learn how to use the Computer-Based-Test system, mark questions and go back to them at the end of your exam. You will have 15 minutes to go through this tutorial.

If you are familiar in the use of computers (Linux, Mac, or PC), you will definitively not need the full 15 minutes to finish this tutorial. But, don't waste this valuable time to rush into the exam. Instead, I advise you to perform a 5 to 7 minute brain dump!

The day of the exam, before sitting in front of your testing computer, you will be provided with a 6-page scrap paper and 2 pencils. Use this scrap paper to perform your brain dump.

Exercise: I write-down all the formulas...

The Step #7 helped you in understanding key formulas that you will most certainly need to pass your PMP Certification. Thus, in this first brain dump exercise, your objective should be to write-down all these formulas on paper in 2 to 3 minutes.

Which formulas to write-down in this brain dump?

All the ones you memorized; e.g.: AC, PV, EV, SV, SPI, EAC, ETC, VAC, CV, CPI, BAC, TCPI, SYD Depreciation, Mean, Median, Mode, Standard Deviations, Sigma Values, Probably of A and B, Probably of A or B, etc. And since there are many more formulas applicable to the project management discipline, you may have to time-box this formula brain dump and focus on the formulas that are most challenging to you.

Ready to give it a try?

My Formula Brain Dump: _____

_____

_____

_____

_____

_____

_____

_____

_____

_____

_____

_____

_____

_____

_____

_____

_____

_____

_____

_____

Exercise: I write-down all the processes...

The Step #8 demonstrated how easy it was to remember the 47 project management processes. It's now time to apply this methodology and write-down all 47 processes and their relationships with process groups and knowledge areas.

Your objective should be to generate the below table in less than 3 to 4 minutes.

	Initiating (2)	Planning (24)	Executing (8)	Monitoring & Controlling (11)	Closing (2)
4. Integration	4.1: Develop Project Charter	4.2: Develop Project Management Plan	4.3: Direct and Manage Project Work	4.4: Monitor & Control Project Work 4.5: Perform Integrated Change Control	4.6: Close Project or Phase
5. Scope		5.1: Plan Scope Management 5.2: Collect Requirements 5.3: Define Scope 5.4: Create WBS		5.5: Validate Scope 5.6: Control Scope	
6. Time		6.1: Plan Schedule Management 6.2: Define Activities 6.3: Sequence Activities 6.4: Estimate Activity Resources 6.5: Estimate Activity Duration 6.6: Develop Schedule		6.7: Control Schedule	
7. Cost		7.1: Plan Cost Management 7.2: Estimate Costs 7.3: Determine Budget		7.4: Control Costs	

	Initiating (2)	Planning (24)	Executing (8)	Monitoring & Controlling (11)	Closing (2)
8. Quality		8.1: Plan Quality Management	8.2: Perform Quality Assurance	8.3: Control Quality	
9. Human Resource		9.1: Plan Human Resource Management	9.2: Acquire Project Team 9.3: Develop Project Team 9.4: Manage Project Team		
10. Communica-tions		10.1: Plan Communication Management	10.2: Manage Communications	10.3: Control Communications	
11. Risks		11.1: Plan Risk Management 11.2: Identify Risks 11.3: Perform Qualitative Risk Analysis 11.4: Perform Quantitative Risk Analysis 11.5: Plan Risk Responses		11.6: Control Risks	
12. Procurement		12.1: Plan Procurement	12.2: Conduct Procurements	12.3: Control Procurements	12.4: Close Procurement
13. Stakeholder	13.1: Identify Stakeholder	13.2: Plan Stakeholder Management	13.3: Manage Stakeholder Engagement	13.4: Control Stakeholder Engagement	

If you have memorized all the key formulas and the above mapping, you should still have 5 minutes left before the clock stops ticking. Use these remaining minutes wisely: Breathe, calm down, and remember you have done everything right. You have no reason to feel nervous.

Step #12: Prepare the Final Logistics

Let's step back, and get ahead of ourselves: it's not D Day yet. If you have followed the proposed schedule, you are still four days away from passing the PMP Certification.

While you complete your learning objectives, take a final PMP Exam simulation, and train for the 5-minute brain dump, I want you to gain additional insights into the exam and how it would be on D Day.

I have already covered a couple of points in the previous steps, but let me give you a better idea of what you should prepare yourself for, before, during and after taking the exam.

Locate the Testing Center

A couple of days before taking the exam, unless you are very family with the location of your testing center, I would recommend you to map the testing center and, drive there at the approximate time your appointment is scheduled. And if you don't plan on driving but, taking the public transportation, study the bus or subway routes, and experience the voyage to your destination.

Either way, this will give you a better idea of how long it will take you to go to the testing center, and help you ensure an early arrival on test day.

Arrive Early On the Day of Exam

If your test is scheduled at 8am, because Prometric Testing Centers offer a wide-range of computer-based tests, you may have to wait in line to sign up. It's not rare to have more than 30 people scheduled at the same time as you.

Thus, even though arriving an hour early may sound like too much, you will ultimately avoid unnecessary stress; wondering if you would be able to sign-up and be placed at your desk on time. Plus, by arriving and signing-up early, you will have plenty of time to:
1. Place all your personal items into the small locker you will be assigned to, and
2. Stop by the washroom before being escorted to your seat...

The above bullets do imply 2 important things:

1. You cannot bring any personal items (cellphone, wallet, keys, watch, etc.) into the testing room
2. You will not be allowed to enter or leave the testing room without being escorted.

The latter also means that each time you want to leave the testing room, you will have to sign out with the attendant who will then escort you to do your business. Finally, to get back into the testing room, you will have to show your ID, and sign back with the attendant, before sitting at your desk again.

Thus, let me emphasize it one more time: **arrive early!**

Sign-up

Before leaving your house or office, and head to the testing center, don't forget to bring:

1. At least 2 government-issued identification cards (driver license, valid passport, green card, military ID, etc.). The ID must contain your full name, your photo and your signature
2. Your scheduling notification, which includes you unique PMI Identification code; you should have received this notification when you set and schedule your appointment
3. A light vest

As you arrive in the testing center, you will be asked to sign-in. Both ID and your appointment notice are required. Your identification must match your name as it appears on your scheduling notification. If the name on your identification and scheduling notification does not exactly match, you will not be permitted to test, and will have to pay the re-examination fee in order to reschedule...

You will then wait to be called to complete the registration process. Once you are called, and have signed-up, don't forget to request a small locker to leave all your personal belongings there, make a pit stop as need be, and here you go!

Oh, yes, I forget: why bringing a light vest? Because the testing room may be a little chilly and you don't want to lose your concentration because of being cold... Simple question, simple answer!

Enter the Testing Room

After signing-up, you will be escorted into the testing room. You will be given 6 sheets of paper, 2 pencils, and if you ask, a small calculator as well.

You will be escorted to your seat, where the attendant will initiate the session for you to follow the now famous 15-minute tutorial. Use these 15 minutes wisely: remember the brain dump exercises!

Once you complete your brain dump, and confirm you have completed the instructions of tutorial, you will have 60 seconds to start the test...

Take the Test

The exam consists of 200 multiple choice questions. 25 of the 200 questions are "*sample*" questions and are not counted for or against you. These questions are placed randomly throughout the exam. You will be graded on the remaining 175 questions.

Once you start the test, you have 4 hours to complete it. If you take a break, the clock does not stop. Hence, if you need a break, knowing the process to get in and out of the testing room, my advice is to stay at your desk, close your eyes, breathe deeply, move your shoulder and neck, relax a few seconds, and get back into it!

As you take the test or a short break at your desk, beware that you are not allowed to talk or put your hands in your pocket.

Note as well that you will not be alone in the testing room, and the PMP is not necessary the exam the other candidates are taking. The exam they take may only last an hour or two. This means that people will come and go around you.

So, be prepared, and don't let them disturb you.

Stay focused!

At last, remember all the other tips we discussed earlier:

1. Be aware of time, and don't spend too much time on one question! you have 200 questions to answer in 4 hours; this means, you have a little more than 1 minute per question
2. Pace yourself! Taking a 4-hour exam can be intense and stressful. Leverage the first 3 hours to go through as many questions as you can (if not all), and during the last hour, go back the questions you were unsure or did not respond to
3. Take your time reading carefully the question, especially if this is a scenario question
4. Many questions are designed to be long and made to confuse you, So always ask yourself what the real question is, and most of the time, the last sentence includes the real question
5. Don't read more into a question; there is no trick
6. When you are not sure about an answer, first eliminate the obviously wrong answers, and pick one; if you can eliminate 2 answers, you have increase your chance by 50%
7. Don't leave any questions unanswered! Leaving a question blank always leads to 0. Hence, even if you don't know, just guess; you still have 25% of chance to answer correctly
8. Do the simple math in your head, but if you are uncertain, do the calculations on paper!

And if I may add: try to have fun!

Complete the Test

After answering and reviewing the 200 questions, you will be asked to click on a *"complete exam"* button.

A confirmation dialog box will then prompt you *"are you sure?"*

If you select yes, the system will calculate immediately your results. Fifteen to twenty seconds later, you should hopefully read on the screen: *"you passed."*

You can now ask the attendant to escort you out of the testing room. The attendant will however first carefully check if you have returned all the items provided before the exam: calculator, pencils and, scrap paper. You won't be able to keep any of your notes.

At last, the attendant will print your score, showing your proficiency in each process group area, and will hand you a certified copy of your test results.

Step #13: Stop Studying and Sleep Well

Now that you have been able to get a glimpse at the testing center, and better understand what to expect during the exam, don't you think it's time to relax? After all, tomorrow is D Day! And, the last thing you want before taking an exam is to have a stressful evening!

Hence, my last tip is the simplest one: stop studying and have a resting night! Have a peaceful night is your best allies. It will wash your stress away, and help you arrive refreshed the next day.

Naturally, to sleep well, try to have a stress-free day the day before. If you plan on taking the exam during the weekdays, consider taking a day-off; you want to empty your mind, and avoid any sources of distraction and stress. Try as well to eat familiar food, something you like and can digest easily...

So, have a good night, and see you bright and ready tomorrow morning!

Step #14: Start your Exam with Confidence

Today is D Day!

The last few weeks, with hard work and continuous dedication, you did everything right!

You defined your learning objectives. You planned and studied with intelligence. You read the *PMBOK® Guide*, understood the PMI's perspective on the project management processes, and did not uniquely rely on your own experience. You simulated many times the exams, and adjusted your learning objectives based on continuous self-feedback and the scoring of the simulated exams. And, as D Day approached, you learned what to expect and prepared yourself, putting all the required paperwork near your keys and wallet.

In short, you did not take lightly the PMP Exam, and are now about to complete this long journey. Trust me, you are ready to tackle the exam questions with confidence!

As you head to the testing center, think positively, and visualize the last dialog box you will see after completing the exam: *"you passed."* The rest is simple; it's about going to the motion: signing-up, making a pit stop, being escorted into the testing room, adjusting your chair to be as comfortable as possible, going through the tutorial, completing your brain dump, focusing the remaining 4 hours, and just like that, you will receive in your inbox your certification!

Step #15: Join the PMI Community

Congratulations, you just have passed the PMP Exam!

You are now officially a Certified Project Manager for the next 3 years.

Your PMP certification is indeed valid for 3 years only. And, it's up to you to keep your status in good standing. To do so, you will need to participate in professional development activities to earn 60 Professional Development Units (PDUs) over the next 3 years, hence maintaining your credential.

The reason why I suggest you to join the PMI is that as a member, you will gain exclusive access to PMI publications, networking options, online communities of practice, and more importantly, you will be able to attend free webinars; one webinar allowing to gain 1 PDU. Additionally, you'll receive discounts on professional development offerings and continuous education training materials.

As you complete a training qualifying for one to many PDUs, as a PMI member, you will have the opportunity to report your PDUs online, removing any challenging administrative roadblocks. At last, as a PMI member, you will be able to access many free resources to jumpstart your own projects: Tools and Templates, and a surprisingly extended project management knowledge database.

So, don't wait, and join the PMI Community today: http://www.pmi.org

And Then?

Once again, congratulations!

Congratulations on successfully completing this journey.

Congratulations on passing your PMP Certification!

This road was not an easy one, but you managed to overcome all challenges placed in front you. You stayed engaged and motivated, and continued your way till passing your certification, thus reaching your earlier objective.

You can now close the page of this chapter of your life and, start writing a new one!

What to do? Where to go?

The choice is yours!

But, remember the first step of this journey, remember the questions I was asking you:
- What motivates you?
- Why do you wish to pass your PMP Certification?
- Do you remember the mission statement you defined for yourself?

If so, write it down again!

It is my mission to: _____

_____

_____

_____

Face it! Passing the PMP Certification was only a first step toward achieving your lifelong objectives.

So, what's next? What do you want to do next?

The Road is yours to take.

Bonus: 200-Question Practice Exam

This exam includes 200 questions that should prepare you getting ready for your exam. Some of these questions are from The Project Management Test Bank, which was established in 2009 and rebranded in 2011 the vision of providing free and beneficial resources to all Project Management practitioners.

Question #1
_____ is developing an approximation of the costs of the resources needed to complete project activities.

A: Resource planning

B: Cost estimating

C: Cost budgeting

D: Cost control

Question #2
_____ involve(s) coordinating people and other resources to carry out the plan

A: Work breakdown structure

B: Resource planning

C: Planning processes

D: Executing processes

Question #3

_____ is controlling changes to the budget.

A: Resource planning

B: Cost estimating

C: Cost budgeting

D: Cost control

Question #4

_____ is ensuring all features and functions are included in a product or service:

A: Project scope

B: Project verification

C: Project control

D: Product scope

Question #5

_____ involves determining what quantities are to be used to perform project activities.

A: Resource planning

B: Cost estimating

C: Cost budgeting

D: Cost control

Question #6

_____ must be measured regularly to identify variances from the plan.

A: Stakeholder requirements

B: Project performance

C: Schedule control

D: Project controls

Question #7

_____ recognizes that a project or phase should begin and commits the organization to do so

A: Initiating process

B: Solicitation process

C: Scoping process

D: Planning process

Question #8

_____ includes the process required to ensure that the project includes all the work required, and only the work required, to complete the project successfully.

A: Project plan update

B: Project scope management

C: Scope change control

D: Product description

Question #9

A _____ is a series of actions bringing about a result.

A: Project plan

B: Process

C: Schedule

D: Flowchart

Question #10

A company has to make a choice between two projects, because the available resources in money and kind are not sufficient to run both at the same time. Each project would take 9 months and would cost $250,000. 1) The first project is a process optimization which would result in a cost reduction of $120,000 per year. This benefit would be achieved immediately after the end of the project. 2) The second project would be the development of a new product which could produce the following net profits after the end of the project: 1. year: $15,000, 2. year: $125,000, 3. year: $220,000. Assumed is a discount rate of 5% per year.

Looking at the present values of the benefits of these projects in the first 3 years, what is true?

A: Both projects are equally attractive

B: The first project is more attractive by app. 7%

C: The second project is more attractive by app. 5%

D: The first project is more attractive by app. 3%

Question #11

A contingency plan is executed when:

A: A risk is identified

B: An identified risk occurs

C: When a workaround is needed

D: All of the above

Question #12

A contingency plan is:

A: A planned response that defines the steps to be taken if an identified risk event should occur

B: A workaround

C: A reserve used to allow for future situations which may be planned for only in part

D: A and C

Question #13

A contract where the buyer reimburses the seller for the cost incurred by the seller, and also provides for a fixed amount of profit is also called:

A: Cost Plus Incentive Fee

B: Cost Plus Fixed Fee

C: Time and Material Contract

D: Cost Plus Percentage of cost

Question #14
A document or tool which describes when and how human resources will be brought onto and taken off the project team is called a:

A: Staffing Management Plan

B: Responsibility Assignment Matrix (RAM)

C: Organizational Breakdown Structure (OBS)

D: Resource Assignment Chart

Question #15
A key barrier to team development is:

A: When team members are accountable to both functional and project managers

B: A strong matrix management structure

C: When major problems delay the project completion date or budget targets

D: When formal training plans cannot be implemented

Question #16
A process that is not part of Project Risk Management is:

A: Identification

B: Sollicitation

C: Quantification

D: Response Development

Question #17
A program is defined in the PMBOK as:

A: A group of projects managed in a coordinated way to obtain benefits not available from managing them individually

B: A number of subprojects divided into manageable components enabling a project team to ensure the completion of a desired outcome

C: A project plan developed by key management personnel to obtain a desired outcome

D: The means to subdivide the project into manageable segments

Question #18
A project can best be defined as:

A: Series of non-related activities designed to accomplish single and multiple objectives

B: Coordinated effort of related activities designed to accomplish a goal without a well-established end point

C: Cradle-to-grave activities which must be accomplished in less than one year and consumes human and non-human resources

D: "Any undertaking with a definable time frame, well-defined objectives, and consumes both human and non-human resources with certain constraints."

Question #19

A project Manager has to manage conflict in an organization. All the following could be sources of conflict in an organization EXCEPT:

A: Weak Matrix Structure with multiple managers to report to

B: Low position in the organization hierarchy

C: Roles that are not well defined

D: Work pressure and high stress

Question #20

A Project Manager must have good understanding of the mechanics of power and politics to be effective. As defined by Pfeffer, power includes all the following EXCEPT:

A: The potential to influence behavior

B: Potential to change the course of events and overcome resistance

C: Ability to get people to do things that they would not otherwise do

D: Ability to handle power struggles and organizational games

Question #21

A RAM is defined as:

A: Random access memory

B: Rapid air movement

C: Responsibilities and methods

D: Responsibility assignment matrix

Question #22
A resource pool description provides:

A: The unit cost for each resource

B: What are the resources are available, at what times and in what patterns

C: Performance of the pool resources

D: Duration of the project

Question #23
A risk response which involves eliminating a threat is called:

A: Mitigation

B: Deflection

C: Avoidance

D: Transfer

Question #24
A scope management plan describes:

A: An assessment of the stability of the stakeholder environment

B: A highly detailed approach to managing the work breakdown structure scope

C: How the project scope will be managed and how scope changes will be integrated into the project

D: The stake holder's expectation on how changes will be identified and by what priority they will be addressed

Question #25
A WBS should be developed to cover

A: As many level of detail you want to

B: Up to 3 level of detail and 80 hrs.

C: What your manager feel comfortable with

D: The number needed to control the project effectively

Question #26
A work breakdown structure is a:

A: Result of the scope planning process

B: Deliverable oriented grouping of project elements that organizes and defines the total scope of the project

C: Structure that can be used to track the project's time, cost, and quality performance against a defined baseline

D: Valuable communications tool, but cannot be used to establish the number of required networks for cost control

Question #27
According to Herzbergs theory, all the following are motivating agents EXCEPT:

A: Recognition

B: Responsibility

C: Advancement in career

D: Salary

Question #28

According to the 80/20 rule, 80 percent of the problems are because of 20 percent of the causes. To facilitate finding out which are the most probable defects, you do a rank ordering of the defects using:

A: Statistical Sampling

B: Control Chart

C: Pareto Diagrams

D: Inspection

Question #29

Actual cost=$1000, Budget at completion=$800, cost performance index=0.5, Earned value= $600, the variance can occur again. The estimate at completion is:

A: $1000

B: $1400

C: $800

D: None of the above

Question #30

All direct or indirect training costs should generally be the responsibility of the:

A: Program Office of the Project

B: Project budget (hence paid from the project sizing)

C: Performing organization

D: Project Sponsor and Business partner

Question #31
All of the following are outputs of the close project process EXCEPT:

A: Historical information

B: Project management plan updates

C: Project closure documents

D: Formal acceptance documentation

Question #32
All of the following are true concerning the product description except

A: it is another term for the Statement of Work (SOW)

B: it describes the ultimate end product of the project

C: it provides important information about any technical issues that are relevant to procurement planning

D: it is usually included in the Request for Proposal (RFP)

Question #33
All the following are conflict resolution modes EXCEPT:

A: Collaborating

B: Smoothing

C: Avoiding

D: Directing

Question #34
All the following are responsibilities of a certified PMP EXCEPT:

A: Ensure that there is no conflict of interest that can compromise the legitimate interests of a client or customer

B: Ensure that the technical specifications are appropriately defined

C: Disseminate PMP Code of Professional Conduct to other PMI certificants

D: Cooperate with PMI concerning ethics violation and the collection of related information

Question #35
All the following are tools and techniques for organization planning EXCEPT:

A: Templates

B: Human Resource Practices

C: Organizational Theory

D: Reward and Recognition Systems

Question #36
All the following are tools for cost estimating EXCEPT:

A: Analogous Estimating

B: Parametric Modeling

C: Computerized tools

D: Alternatives Identification

Question #37
All the following are true about contract negotiation EXCEPT:

A: Primary objective should be to build a lasting relationship

B: It includes responsibilities, contract financing, technical and business management approaches

C: Price is an important consideration during Negotiation

D: Main consideration of both buyer and seller should be to maximize monetary return

Question #38
All the following are true about Project Execution EXCEPT:

A: Vast majority of the project budget will be expended in Project Plan Execution

B: Project Manager and her team coordinate the various technical and organizational interfaces

C: Product of the project is created

D: Care is taken to ensure that changes to the product scope are reflected in the project scope

Question #39
All the following statements about Cost Baseline are correct EXCEPT:

A: It is a time phased budget

B: To measure disbursements, a spending plan can be used as a cost-baseline

C: It is used to measure and monitor project performance

D: All projects have one cost baseline

Question #40
All the following statements relating to communication management are correct EXCEPT:

A: Communication Planning involves determining the information and communication needs of the stakeholders

B: Communicating is the most critical skill that a project manager should possess

C: Project Managers spend as more than 85% of their time communicating

D: To be effective, a Project Manager should control all communications

Question #41
All the following statements relating to transferring of risk to a contractor are true EXCEPT:

A: Transferring risk requires payment of a risk premium

B: Fixed price contracts transfer risk to the seller if the design is unstable

C: Cost reimbursable contract leaves more of the risk with the customer or sponsor

D: Cost reimbursable contract helps reduce cost if there are mid-project changes

Question #42
All the following tools and techniques can be used for staff acquisition EXCEPT:

A: Negotiations

B: Contractual agreements with unions or other employee groups

C: Preassignment of staff through a competitive proposal

D: Staff assignment as defined in the project charter

Question #43

An accepted deadline for a project approaches. However, the project manager realizes only 75% percent of the work has been completed. The project manager then issues a change request.

What should the change request authorize?

A: Additional resources using the contingency fund

B: Escalation approval to use contingency funding

C: Team overtime to meet schedule

D: Corrective action based on causes

Question #44

An output of the scope change control process is:

A: Scope statement

B: Lessons learned

C: Formal acceptance

D: Work breakdown structure

Question #45

As a Project Manager for a construction company, you are responsible for Scope Definition, Activity Definition, Schedule Development and Cost Budgeting.

These responsibilities are performed as part of:

A: Closing

B: Concept

C: Planning

D: Execution

Question #46

As a project manager of a construction company, you always prefer to do concrete curing during the weekend holiday, because no work can be done on the building for 2 days while the concrete curing is being done.

This helps you decrease the:

A: Waiting Time

B: Elapsed Time

C: Project Schedule

D: Critical Path

Question #47

As a project Manager, Problem solving is high in your list of priorities. Which statement about Problem Solving is not accurate?

A: Problem solving involves a combination of problem definition and decision-making

B: Problems may be technical, managerial or interpersonal

C: Decision Making includes analyzing the problem to identify viable solutions, and then making a choice from among them

D: You should try to solve a problem as soon as it is identified

Question #48

As a project manager, you advocate active participation of your team members - this is because you believe in:

A: Theory Y (McGregor Model)

B: Theory X (McGregor Model)

C: Maslow hierarchy of needs

D: Referent power

Question #49
As a Project Manager, you have to manage the project and lead the team in delivering a successful project. Managing is primarily concerned with:

A: Consistently producing key results expected by stakeholders

B: Establishing direction

C: Motivating and inspiring

D: Aligning people

Question #50
As a Project Manager, you realize that it is very important to be a good leader. Leading involves all the following EXCEPT:

A: Consistently producing key results expected by stakeholders

B: Establishing direction

C: Aligning people

D: Motivating and Inspiring

Question #51
As part of a successful communication, the receiver is responsible for:

A: Making sure the information is clear and complete, understood and acknowledged

B: Making sure the information is received in its entirety, understood correctly and acknowledged

C: Making sure the information is clear and complete, understood and agreed with

D: Listening actively to ensure all of the information is received

Question #52

Bob's project is behind schedule. Bob opens his project scheduling tool and adjusts some leads and lags in order to fast track the project. As a result, the project is aligned with the current time constraint. However, when Bob uses the Level Resources feature of scheduling tool, the project completion date again goes past the time constraint. What is Bob's best option?

A: Bob must make sure that he did not make a mistake when using the Level Resources feature

B: Bob must not use the Level Resources feature after fast tracking the project

C: Bob must crash the project after fast tracking it

D: Bob must speak with the customer and issue a change request

Question #53

Characteristics of project phases are:

A: Milestones

B: Deliverables

C: Activities

D: All of the above

Question #54
Collocation can mean:

A: All, or almost all, team members are moved to a central physical location for the life of the project

B: Active team members may be at different physical locations, but meet on a regular basis

C: A war room is established where team members can meet periodically

D: a and c

Question #55
Completion of the _____ scope is measured against the plan.

A: Project

B: Technical

C: Product

D: Baseline

Question #56
Constraints do not include:

A: Impacts of weather

B: Organizational structure of the performing organization

C: Collective bargaining

D: Expected staff assignments

Question #57

Contingency planning is a means to _____ risks to the project through a formal process and provides the resources to meet the risk events.

A: Address

B: Classify

C: Assign

D: Resolve

Question #58

Contract Negotiation is carried out as part of:

A: Plan Procurements Management

B: Source Selection

C: Conduct Procurements

D: Control Procurements

Question #59

Decomposition is

A: What happens when changes to the project scope are ignored?

B: Subdividing the major project deliverables into smaller, more manageable components

C: Defining a general product description into more discrete definitions of individual components

D: Subdividing the project into logical divisions of effort aligned within the performing organization's functional areas

Question #60

Developing a written scope statement as the basis for future project decisions is called:

A: Product analysis

B: Scope definition

C: Project development

D: Scope planning

Question #61

During a meeting with some of your project's stakeholders, you are asked to add to the project's scope of work. The project records contain correspondence from before the Charter was signed in which the project sponsor specifically declined the work being requested by these stakeholders.

The best thing for you to dis:

A: Tell the stakeholders the work cannot be added

B: Evaluate the cost and time impacts of adding the work

C: Add the work if it can be accommodated within the existing budget

D: Talk to the sponsor and let her know of the request

Question #62

For a project to be successful, what is the primary requirement?

A: Customer Satisfaction

B: Exceeding Customer Requirements

C: Meeting the cost and schedule estimates

D: Satisfying the requirements of the project sponsor

Question #63
General Management encompasses all but:

A: Finance and accounting

B: Strategic planning

C: Sales and marketing

D: Developing a new product or service

Question #64
Group brainstorming encourages all of the following EXCEPT:

A: Team building

B: Analysis of alternatives

C: Convergent thinking

D: Uninhibited verbalization

Question #65
Historical record from previous project are generally used for all of the following EXCEPT:

A: Lessons learned

B: Estimating

C: Risk management

D: Project planning

Question #66
If a project has an 80% chance of having the scope defined by a certain date and a 70% chance of obtaining approval for the scope by a certain date, what is the probability of both events occurring?

A: 0.75

B: 0.65

C: 0.5

D: 0.56

Question #67
If a property depreciates by the same amount every year, it is called:

A: Sum of the Year Digits

B: Accelerated Depreciation

C: Straight Line Depreciation

D: Double Declining Balance

Question #68
If there is a change to the approved cost baseline, the project manager must:

A: Issue a Budget Update

B: Perform Rebaselining

C: Issue a Revised Cost Estimate

D: Take Corrective Action

Question #69
If you are calculating one early start and early finish for each task, you are using: (choose the BEST answer)

A: PERT

B: CPM

C: GERT

D: PDM

Question #70
In a Lump-sum contract, the profit is:

A: Determined by the buyer during contract sign-off

B: Determined by the seller during contract sign-off

C: Provided by the buyer to the seller at end of project if defined performance criteria are met

D: Not known at time of the contract sign-off

Question #71
In a project lifecycle, least number of conflicts occur over:

A: Priorities

B: Schedules

C: Personality Conflict

D: Cost

Question #72

In a project, you are presented with following four options. Which project should you select?

A: Project A with Opportunity Cost of $ 100,000

B: Project B with Benefit-Cost Ratio of 0.75

C: Project C with IRR of -2%

D: Project D with NPV of $ 100,000

Question #73

In a sender-receiver model, all the following are true EXCEPT:

A: Sender is responsible for making information clear, unambiguous and complete

B: Sender confirms that information is understood

C: Receiver is responsible for making sure that the information is completely received and understood

D: All the statement above are true

Question #74

In an automobile company for which you are the project manager, the allowable standard deviation for a product required from the contractor is within 0.002 inches. However, while examining the product, you find out that the standard deviation is slightly more than 0.002 inches. You believe that the deviation is very small and hence, acceptable. In this case you must:

A: Allow the product because it is a very small deviation from the company standard which you think is acceptable

B: Document the lower quality level, ask the contractor for explanation and try to find a solution

C: Reject the product outright

D: Allow the lower standard this time but inform the contractor to be more quality conscious going forward

Question #75

In order to anticipate your management's approval of the amount of risk you plan to take on with your chosen project approach, you would use _____

A: Probability analysis

B: The Delphi method

C: The Monte Carlo method

D: The utility theory

Question #76
In schedule development, mathematical analysis often produces a preliminary early-start schedule that shows peaks and valleys in the resource requirements. Resource Leveling done to take care of this issue may result in all the following EXCEPT:

A: Increase in project duration

B: Utilization of weekends, extended hours or multiple shifts

C: Productivity increases by using different technologies and/or methodologies

D: Reduction in project cost

Question #77
In which of the following contract types is the seller's profit limited?

A: Cost-plus-percentage-cost contract

B: Cost-plus-fixed-fee contract

C: Fixed-price-plus-incentive

D: b and c

Question #78
In your company, for making investment decisions, the senior management prefers to use a rate that equates present value of cash inflows with present value of cash outflows. This can also be called:

A: Discount Rate

B: Benefit Cost Ratio

C: Internal Rate of Return

D: Net Present Value

Question #79

In your construction project, the CPI is 0.85 and SPI is 1.25.

What could be the potential reason?

A: A critical resource went on sick leave for a long period of time, which had not been anticipated earlier

B: The cost of raw materials required for construction increased 1.0% - you had anticipated a cost increase of 1.2% in your project plans

C: Anticipating delays, the project had to be crashed to decrease duration

D: There was 4 days waiting time in the curing of cement, and work could not be done during that time

Question #80

In your construction project, you decide to make a small change to the height of a flyover. Small changes to the height of a flyover is mentioned in your change control system is a change that will allow for "automatic approval." In this case, you should:

A: Submit your change request to the group responsible for approving or rejecting changes

B: Since this is a small change, you go ahead and make the change without any documentation

C: Must mandatorily make changes to the cost and budget estimates

D: Document the change and go ahead with implementing the change because no approvals are required

Question #81

In your new company, you realize that some of the financial statements of the company do not follow US GAAP Accounting Standards and are hence inaccurate. In this case, what should you do first?

A: Inform the US government agencies of the inaccurate accounting practices in the company

B: Talk to your finance managers about why you think that they may be violating the standard accounting standards

C: Since you are new to the company, you assume that finance standards are different in the company - hence do not do anything about the issue

D: Talk with finance manager in your previous company to get expert opinion about accounting standards in the new company

Question #82

In your previous project, the project manager gave a lot of autonomy to the team members to do as they deemed fit. At times, this lead to anarchy because the team members were not very sure of what needed to be done. The manager however followed a management style, which was:

A: Directing

B: Laissez Faire

C: Delegating

D: Democratic

Question #83

In your project, a team member suggested the addition of a functionality to improve customer satisfaction. Your approach would be to:

A: Allow for the functionality because satisfying the customer is your objective

B: Do not allow for the new requirement, because it will be a change in scope, and the customer did not explicitly mention the requirement

C: Make changes to the project plan to accommodate the new requirement

D: Ask the customer for additional funding for implementing the requirement

Question #84

In your project, you are creating a diagram that describes the decision under consideration and implications of choosing one or another of the available alternatives. This will help in:

A: Getting a Qualitative Analysis of the risk

B: Determining which risks can impact the project the most

C: Translating the uncertainties at a detailed level into potential impact on objectives expressed at the level of the total project

D: Determining which decision yields the greatest expected value

Question #85

In your software project, you have a programmer who constantly professes to know all about project management, and keeps challenging his superiors. The programmer is playing the role of a (an):

A: Aggressor

B: Conflict Maxi miser

C: Devil's advocate

D: Dominator

Question #86

Key Management skills include:

A: Leading

B: Communicating

C: Negotiating

D: All of the above

Question #87

Management reserves are used to handle which type of risk?

A: Unknown unknowns

B: Known unknowns

C: business risks

D: pure risks

Question #88

_____ must be measured regularly to identify variance from the plan.

A: Stakeholder requirements

B: Project performance

C: Schedule progress

D: Cost and schedule

Question #89

One of your friends is a manager at Telecommunications Company. She is currently managing a project developing a VoIP (Voice over IP) gateway that addresses the challenges facing service providers deploying packer-based voice networks. The gateway offers a comprehensive approach to implementing high-density carrier-class voice over packet gateway applications. All the technical work has already been completed on the project, and the project is in the closing phase. All of the following should be performed at this stage EXCEPT:

A: Analyze the success or failure of the project

B: Documents lessons learned

C: Perform product verification

D: Obtain formal acceptance of the project scope and deliverables

Question #90

Outputs from the initiation process are:

A: Project manager identified/assigned

B: Constraints

C: Assumptions

D: All of the above

Question #91
Performance improvements include all but:

A: Improvements in amount of overtime worked

B: Improvements in individual skills

C: Improvements in team behaviors

D: Improvements in team capabilities

Question #92
Please refer to this Decision Tree which shows the analysis of profit/loss for the two alternatives (i.e. to build or buy).

What should the project Manager recommend?

A: Build

B: Buy

C: Either Build or Buy

D: Project Manager should recommend a Sensitivity Analysis before making a build/buy decision

Question #93
Project Integration Management

A: Describes the processes required to ensure that the project includes all the work required to complete the project successfully

B: Describes the processes required to ensure timely completion of the project

C: Describes the processes required to ensure that the project will satisfy the needs for which it was undertaken

D: Describes the processes required to ensure that the various elements of the project are properly coordinated

Question #94
Project risk is characterized by three factors:

A: Severity of impact, duration of impact and cost of impact

B: Identification, type of risk category and probability of impact

C: Risk event, risk probability and the amount at stake

D: Occurrence, frequency and cost

Question #95
Project risk is defined as the cumulative effect of chances of _____ which will adversely affect project objectives.

A: Likely events

B: Complex activities

C: Complex schedules

D: Uncertain occurrences

Question #96
Project Risk Management includes all of the following processes EXCEPT:

A: Risk Quantification

B: Risk Identification

C: Risk Analysis

D: Risk Response Development

Question #97
Project Scope Management includes which processes:

A: Initiation

B: Project Plan Execution

C: Overall Change Control

D: Performance Reporting

Question #98
Project selection criteria cover management concerns such as:

A: Financial return

B: Market share

C: Public perception

D: All of the above

Question #99
Project Stakeholders are defined as:

A: Individuals and organizations who use the project's product

B: Individuals and organizations whose interest may be positively or negatively affected as a result of project execution or successful project completion

C: Individuals and organizations who provide the financial resources

D: All of the above

Question #100
Receipt of bids or proposals and application of the evaluation criteria to select a provider should be done as part of:

A: Procurement Planning

B: Solicitation

C: Solicitation Planning

D: Source Selection

Question #101
Risk event is the precise description of what might happen to the _____ of the project.

A: Manager

B: Detriment

C: Schedule

D: Budget

Question #102
Risk management is defined as the art and science of _____ risk factors throughout the life cycle of a project.

A: Researching, reviewing and acting on

B: Identifying, analyzing and responding to

C: Reviewing, monitoring and managing

D: Identifying, reviewing and avoiding

Question #103
Risks are accepted when:

A: You develop a contingency plan to execute should the risk event occur

B: You accept the consequences of the risk

C: You transfer the risk to another party

D: A and B

Question #104
Risks that remain after avoidance, transfer and mitigation are also called:

A: Unidentifiable Risks

B: Residual Risks

C: Secondary Risks

D: Accepted Risks

Question #105
Scope planning includes alternatives identification, which can be conducted by the common technique of:

A: Lateral thinking

B: Value engineering

C: Cost/benefit analysis

D: Constraints analysis

Question #106
Scope planning is:

A: Developing a comprehensive plan based on input from major stakeholders

B: Developing a written scope statement as the basis for future project decisions

C: The process, which provides information for planning project milestones

D: Subdividing the project into smaller, more manageable components

Question #107
Team Development is a very critical component of Human Resource Management. All the following are inputs to Team Development EXCEPT:

A: Project Plan

B: Project Staff

C: Staffing pool description

D: Performance Report

Question #108
The _____ documents the characteristics of the product or service that the project was undertaken to create.

A: Resource plan

B: Project charter

C: Project description

D: Scope Statement

Question #109

The activity list should include descriptions of activities. This is required to:

A: Provide documented evidence of the scope of work

B: Ensure that the team members understand how the work is to be done

C: Provide as a reminder to the project manager

D: Help in creation of technical documentation during the project life cycle

Question #110

The Close Project or Phase process is a part of which of the following project management knowledge areas?

A: Project Scope Management

B: Project Integration Management

C: Project Time Management

D: Project Communication Management

Question #111

The Control Costs process includes all of the following EXCEPT:

A: Informing appropriate stakeholders of all approved changes and associated costs

B: Influencing factors that create changes in the authorized cost baseline

C: Developing the cost performance baseline

D: Acting to bring expected cost overruns within acceptable limits

Question #112
The core planning processes include:

A: Scope planning, activity sequencing, communications planning

B: Quality planning, communications planning, risk response development

C: Scope definition, activity duration estimating, cost budgeting

D: Scope planning, activity definition, cost estimating, quality planning, risk response planning

Question #113
As the project manager of an important project, you learnt many helpful tools and tips. What should you do?

A: Keep them to yourself

B: Archive your learning in the project folder and share with other PMs

C: Sign a non-disclosure agreement

D: None of the above

Question #114
The cost baseline is usually not changed unless

A: the basis for the original cost estimate is found to be false and the project must be re-estimated

B: significant cost deviations have been reported and it is desired to have future cost reports be based on an as of date

C: the revision is the result of an approved scope change

D: the time baseline is also changed

Question #115
The Delphi Method is best suited for:

A: Decision-making

B: Cost Control

C: Overhead rate estimating

D: Team discussions

Question #116
The documents the characteristics of the product or service that the project was undertaken to create.

A: Project charter

B: Scope statement

C: Product description

D: Technical article

Question #117
The independence of two events in which the occurrence of one is not related to the occurrence of the other is called:

A: event phenomenon

B: independent probability

C: statistical independence

D: statistical probability

Question #118
The items at the lowest level of the WBS are called

A: Code of accounts

B: Subtasks

C: Work packages

D: Nodes

Question #119
The main objective of providing incentives in contracts is to:

A: Align the goals of the buyer and seller

B: Ensure that there is no gold plating

C: Reduce cost for the buyer

D: Improve profits for the seller

Question #120
The main reason to plan team building activities (e.g. regular status review meeting, off-site team meets etc.) is to:

A: Resolve outstanding technical issues

B: Improve Team performance

C: Improve individual morale

D: Relax and get away from the stress of work

Question #121
The one document that should always be used to help identify risk is the:

A: Risk Management Plan

B: WBS

C: Scope Statement

D: Project Charter

Question #122
The outputs from schedule control include all EXCEPT:

A: Schedule updates

B: Revisions

C: Corrective action

D: Lessons learned

Question #123
The outputs from the Control Schedule process include all EXCEPT:

A: Schedule updates

B: Revisions

C: Corrective Action

D: Lessons Learned

Question #124
The process of identifying and defining a product or service is called:

A: Procurement planning

B: Source selection

C: contract execution

D: Contract closeout

Question #125
The project charter has all of the following characteristics EXCEPT:

A: Its primary use is to authorize the start of a project or phase

B: It provides the project manager with authority to apply resources and expend money on project activities

C: Its primary use is to request bids or proposals for the work it defines

D: The project charter can be created by the person external to the project, responsible for the authorization of the work, or that person can delegate the creation of the project charter to the project manager

Question #126
The project team has added some additional functionality which was not required as part of the project. However the customer is satisfied with the project. From a quality perspective:

A: This is high quality because it exceeded customer expectations

B: This is not acceptable quality because gold plating was done which is not advisable

C: This will mean repeat business from the same customer

D: None of the above

Question #127

The responsibility assignment matrix (RAM) shows:

A: The connections between activities and project team members

B: The delegation of responsibility through the hierarchically organized management structure

C: Accountabilities to assist in team performance appraisals.

D: The sequence of activities a named resource is responsible for accomplishing

Question #128

The scope statement should include:

A: Project charter, project objectives and WBS

B: Project objectives, constraints and assumptions

C: Scope of work

D: WBS, work assignment system

Question #129

The sum of the products and services to be provided as a project is called:

A: Scope

B: Deliverables

C: Project charter

D: Data items

Question #130
The three major types of communication are:

A: Written, verbal, and non-verbal

B: Verbal, formal documentation, informal documentation

C: Verbal, written, and graphic

D: Verbal, written, and electronic

Question #131
The tools and techniques used in the initiation process are:

A: Product analysis

B: Project schedule development

C: Expert judgment

D: Project budget

Question #132
The total project scope is:

A: Defined in the project baseline

B: Sum of all the integrated management control plans

C: Sum of the total product scope

D: Constant throughout lifecycle of the project

Question #133
The WBS usually:

A: Define the objectives and assumptions/constraints

B: Determine the project scope

C: Make it easier to assign resources to activity

D: Define the project priorities

Question #134
A comprehensive definition of scope management is

A: approval of scope baseline

B: approval of detailed project charter

C: configuration control

D: managing a project in terms of its objectives through all lifecycle phases and processes

Question #135
The work that must be done in order to deliver a product with the specified features and functions is:

A: Project scope

B: Project verification

C: Project control

D: Product scope

Question #136

There are three projects:

Project A has an investment of $3,000,000 and NPV of $300,000.

Project B has an investment of $2,000,000 payback period of 2 years and NPV of $200,000.

Project C has an investment of $1,000,000 payback period of 2 years and NPV of $100,000.

Which project should be selected if Net Present Value criteria is used for selection?

A: Project A

B: Project B

C: Project C

D: Project A, B or C can be selected because all of them have equal value

Question #137

There have been too many disagreements within two team-members in your project regarding the design of a particular product. You would like to incorporate the best features of the two designs - and want to create an environment that avoids conflicts and emphasis similarities. The conflict-handling mode you would like to emphasize is:

A: Smoothing

B: Compromising

C: Confrontation

D: Withdrawal

Question #138
To determine the tangible and intangible costs and benefits of the project, you will conduct a:

A: Product Analysis

B: Benefit/Cost Analysis

C: Expert Judgment

D: WBS review

Question #139
To identify which quality standards are relevant to a project, and determine how to satisfy them, you will do:

A: Quality Assurance

B: Quality Planning

C: Quality Control

D: Quality Management

Question #140
To manage risks in your project, and communicate with stakeholders, you use several reports. Examples of some reports that could be used include all the following EXCEPT:

A: Issues Log

B: Risk Register

C: Action-item logs

D: Escalation Notices

Question #141

Topics that deal with people include:

A: Leading, communicating, and negotiating with others

B: Delegating, motivating, coaching, mentoring, and other subjects related to dealing with people

C: Performance appraisal, recruitment, retention, labor relations, health and safety regulations, and other subjects related to administering the human resource function

D: All of the above

Question #142

Two project members have been having some disagreement about the best way to handle a problem. You ask both the team members to look at the positives and negatives of both their approaches, and give you their recommendation. Which of the following conflict resolution techniques did you use?

A: Smoothing

B: Compromising

C: Confrontation

D: Withdrawal

Question #143
Under what circumstances is it better for a contractor to subcontract?

A: The subcontractor possesses special technical and engineering skills that the contractor does not have

B: The work to be subcontracted represents almost all of the overall work effort

C: The subcontractor can perform the work at a lower cost than the contractor

D: A and C

Question #144
Using the situation below and assuming continued efficiency for work-in progress and fixed price contract for task four. The estimate at completion is:

A: $19K

B: $21K

C: $26K

D: $29K

Question #145
What is the foundation for team development?

A: Team Building exercises

B: Individual development

C: Appropriate Conflict Management and Resolution

D: Performance Reporting and Evaluation

Question #146
What is the primary role of the project sponsor in a project?

A: Managing the project

B: Using the product of the project

C: Performing work of the project

D: Providing financial resources for the project

Question #147
When managing a complex, cross functional project; which of the following structures will give the project manager the most authority?

A: Balanced matrix

B: Strong matrix

C: Functional

D: Weak matrix

Question #148
When should risk identification be performed? (Select best answer)

A: During Concept Phase

B: During Development Phase

C: During Implementation Phase

D: Risk identification should be performed on a regular basis throughout the project

Question #149
When your objective is to get a lasting win-win solution to a problem, which conflict resolution technique should you use?

A: Collaborating

B: Smoothing

C: Avoiding

D: Withdrawing

Question #150
Which describes how cost variances will be managed?

A: Cost management plan

B: Cost baseline

C: Cost estimate

D: Chart of accounts

Question #151

Which is the best thing to do during the Source Selection process?

A: Determine whether a product should be outsourced or manufactured in-house

B: Ensure that prospective sellers clearly understand the technical and contract requirements

C: Place advertisements in publications

D: Prepare an independent estimate to check the proposed price of the different sellers

Question #152
Which of the following are filters that the receiver uses to filter messages?

A: Language and knowledge

B: Distance

C: Culture and distance

D: Language, distance, culture, and knowledge

Question #153
Which of the following are outputs from the Communications Planning process?

A: Project records

B: Communications management plan

C: Performance reports

D: Formal acceptance

Question #154
Which of the following contract types places the greatest risk on the seller?

A: Cost-plus-fixed-fee contract

B: Cost plus-incentive-fee contract

C: Fixed-price-incentive contract

D: Firm-fixed-price contract

Question #155
Which of the following documents formally indicates that the customer or sponsor has officially accepted the project deliverables?

A: Historical information

B: Formal acceptance documentation

C: Project closure documents

D: Project files

Question #156
Which of the following is an example of constraints?

A: NPV of your project is $5,000

B: IRR can be calculated by internal cash flow

C: Cost of raw material is $30 per unit

D: Government has passed a mandate that your project should not affect the neighborhoods adversely

Question #157
Which of the following is best for handling cross-functional project needs for a large, complex project?

A: A strong matrix organization

B: A project coordinator

C: A project expeditor

D: Direct executive involvement

Question #158
Which of the following is considered during the Procurement Planning Process?

A: Whether to procure

B: How to procure and how much to procure

C: What and when to procure

D: All of the above

Question #159
Which of the following is not a characteristic of the Project Life Cycle?

A: Risk and uncertainty is highest at start of the project

B: Ability of the stakeholders to influence final characteristics of the projects product increases as the project continues

C: The project life cycle definition determines which transitional actions at the beginning and end of the project are included - so, the project life cycle definition can be a link to the ongoing operations of the performing organization

D: Cost and staffing levels are low at the start, higher towards the end and drop rapidly as the project draws to a conclusion

Question #160
Which of the following is not a tool or technique used during the Perform Risk Quantitative Analysis Process?

A: Expected monetary value

B: Contingency planning

C: Decision Trees

D: Statistical sums

Question #161
Which of the following is not an external-unpredictable risk?

A: Changes in government regulations

B: Natural hazards

C: Unexpected environmental side effects

D: Inflation

Question #162
Which of the following is not an input into organizational planning?

A: Recruitment practices

B: Project interfaces

C: Staffing requirements

D: Constraints

Question #163
Which of the following is not an input to Develop Project Charter:

A: Project Statement of Work

B: Enterprise Environmental Factors

C: Organizational Process Assets

D: Project Management Information System

Question #164
Which of the following is the most common non-behavioral reason for projects being completed behind schedule and going over budget?

A: Selecting a wrong person as the project manager

B: Selecting a wrong person as the sponsor

C: Accepting a high-risk project

D: Inadequately defined requirements

Question #165
Which of the following is the most common non-behavioral reason for projects being completed behind schedule and going over budget?

A: Selecting a wrong person as the project manager

B: Selecting a wrong person as the sponsor

C: Accepting a high-risk project

D: Inadequately defined requirements

Question #166
Which of the following methods is least likely to be used for explaining project planning guidelines to the team?

A: Project Office Memo

B: Project office directive

C: Project team meeting

D: Formal project report

Question #167
Which of the following parameter will help in determining probability of getting a result?

A: PERT Value

B: CPM

C: Standard Deviation

D: Variance

Question #168

Which of the following statement related to Standards and Regulations is not correct?

A: Standard is a document approved by a recognized body - there can be multiple standards for one product

B: Regulations are mandatory but Standards are not mandatory

C: Standards after widespread adoption may become de facto regulations

D: The influence of standards and regulations for a project is always known

Question #169

Which of the following statement(s) about project customer and project sponsor is/are correct?

A: Along with the customer, the sponsor threshold for risks should be taken into account

B: Along with the customer, this sponsor may provide key events, milestones, and deliverable due dates

C: Along with the customer, the sponsor formally accepts the product of the project

D: All of the above

Question #170

Which of the following statements are false regarding the administrative closure procedure?

A: The administrative closure procedure is an output of the close project process

B: The administrative closure procedure addresses the terms and conditions of the contract for contract closure

C: The administrative closure procedure addresses the completion or exit criteria for the project

D: The administrative closure procedure describes the procedure to transfer the project products or services to production and/or operations

Question #171

Which of the following statements are true?

A: Procurement audits review the procurement process from plan purchases and acquisition to contract execution

B: Procurement audits review the procurement process from plan purchases and acquisition to close project

C: Procurement audits review the procurement process from plan purchases and acquisition to contract closure

D: Procurement audits review the procurement process from plan contracting to contract closure

Question #172
Which of the following statements relating to Assumptions is inaccurate?

A: They are factors which are considered to be true, real or certain

B: They affect all aspects of project planning,

C: They are progressively elaborated

D: They limit the project team`s options

Question #173
Which of the following techniques accounts for path convergence and generally estimates project durations more accurately?

A: CPM

B: PERT

C: Schedule simulation

D: Path convergence method

Question #174
Which process is not included in Project Cost Management?

A: Closeout

B: Estimating

C: Budgeting

D: Control

Question #175

Which statement describing attributes of the Project Manager is incorrect?

A: General Management Skills (e.g. Leading, Communicating, Negotiating, Problem Solving and Influencing the Organization) provide much of the foundation for building project management skills

B: In projects, the Project Manager is expected to be a leader and be involved with Establishing Direction, Aligning people, Motivating and Inspiring

C: If required, the Project Manager may try to use politics through power struggles or organizational games

D: Project Manager must be aware of and plan for Social-Economic Environmental influences including Standards and Regulations, Internationalization, Cultural Influences and Social-Economic Environmental Sustainability

Question #176

Which statement relating to Core Processes and Facilitating Processes is true?

A: Core processes are mandatory but facilitating processes may be optional

B: Unlike Facilitating processes, core processes have clear dependencies and are performed in same order in most projects

C: Unlike Facilitating processes, interactions between Core processes vary depending on the type of project

D: Core planning processes go through only one iteration, but facilitating processes may undergo multiple iterations

Question #177
While implementing your project, a team member brings to your notice, a risk that was not mentioned in the Risk Response Plan. In this case, you should:

A: Accept the risk

B: Perform Additional Risk Response Planning to control the risk

C: Inform the project sponsor

D: Use project contingency

Question #178
While obtaining responses from prospective sellers, you mention that you will "Require certified PMPs as project managers for the project." This is an example of:

A: Objective Evaluation Criteria

B: Subjective Evaluation Criteria

C: Procurement Documents

D: Statement of Work

Question #179
Work Breakdown Structure is:

A: Developed in the Scope Planning Phase

B: A deliverable oriented grouping of project components

C: Similar to the chart of accounts

D: Depicts work elements assigned to different organizational units

Question #180

You are aware that an employee in your project may potentially get a promotion - however, there is a possibility that he may get transferred after his promotion, thus impacting your project. In this situation, you should:

A: Give a bad recommendation about the person so as to delay the promotion of the person until the project is over

B: Inform the employee about the potential promotion, and ask him to transition his responsibilities to another person

C: After the employee gets the promotion and is told of the transfer, you ask him to prepare a transition plan

D: Hire another resource who can replace the person after he gets the promotion

Question #181

You are in the build phase of the project. But it has run into several unanticipated problems. Several risks have surfaced which you had not anticipated earlier. The project is over-budget and behind schedule. What should you do?

A: Create updates to risk response plan

B: Create a revised project plan

C: Perform risk response audits

D: Perform updated risk identification and analysis

Question #182
You are in the vendor management department of your company which sources computer hardware from companies. You recently went on an official trip to an Asian country to understand the business proposition of a potential vendor. The vendor took you out to lunch and gave you some gifts, as is customary in that country. You must:

A: Tell the vendor that you cannot accept the gifts because of company policy

B: Accept the gift because it is a custom in that country, and also inform your manager

C: Return the gift because it could be construed as personal gain

D: Accept the gift because it is not very expensive

Question #183
You are the project manager for a sewage treatment plant. The government has mandated that you have to ensure that the sewage plant will not adversely impact the neighborhood. From a project perspective, this is a(an):

A: Assumption

B: Constraint

C: Best Practice

D: Deliverable

Question #184

You are the Project Manager for an aircraft manufacturing company developing a new range of supersonic fighter planes. Since government funding is essential for your project, you hire a lobbying firm to get Government support for funding your project. This is an example of:

A: Integrated Change Control

B: Risk Management

C: Cost Management

D: Project Planning Methodology

Question #185

You are the Project Manager responsible for developing a software application based on customer requirements. As the customer requirements keep changing frequently, you use all the following tools for Integrated Change Control EXCEPT:

A: Configuration Management

B: Project Management Information system

C: Corrective Action

D: Additional Planning

Question #186
You are working in the Project Office of your organization. What is your job responsibility?

A: Managing the different activities of a project

B: Always being responsible for the results of the project

C: Providing support functions to Project Managers in the form of training, software, templates etc.

D: Providing Subject Matter Expertise in the Functional areas of the project

Question #187
You began your project with eight total stakeholders. You lost two stakeholders.

How many communications channels were reduced?

A: 28

B: 15

C: 13

D: 43

Question #188
You calculated the mean for your project schedule to be 18 days. Your standard deviation is 2.

What is the potential range for your schedule within 3 Sigma?

A: 18 Days

B: 16 to 20 days

C: 14 to 22 days

D: 12 to 24 days

Question #189
You calculated your standard deviation for a project to be 3.

What is the variance?

A: 6

B: 4

C: 2

D: 9

Question #190
You found the following earned value analysis information for a project that was recently closed-out: SPI = 0.7, CPI = 1.0

A: The project has been cancelled while it was executed. At that time the project was behind schedule and on budget

B: The project's deliverables have all been finished. The project came in behind schedule but budget.

C: The project's deliverables have all been finished. The project came in ahead of schedule but on budget.

D: The project's deliverables have all been finished. The project came in on schedule but over budget

Question #191
You have a five month project with a BAC of $20,000. Funds distribution is linear. You completed month one.

What is your PV?

A: 5000

B: 20000

C: 100000

D: 4000

Question #192

You have a geographically dispersed team, from whom you would like to get expert opinion about your project.

Which information gathering technique should you use?

A: Brainstorming

B: Delphi Technique

C: SWOT Analysis

D: Checklists

Question #193

You have been informed by the project sponsor that there has been a revaluation of projects within your company and your project will not be getting any additional funding. In this case, you should:

A: Stop Work immediately and release all resources

B: Perform Administrative Closure

C: Decrease team size

D: Remove non-critical tasks to decrease cost

Question #194

You purchased a capital asset for $30,000. The asset has a life of four years. How much can you claim for depreciation in year two using the Sum of the Years depreciation technique?

A: 12000

B: 9000

C: 6000

D: 7500

Question #195
Your company has an agreement with the labor union that states that workers will not be asked to work more than 45 hours every week.

For your project, this becomes a:

A: Pre-defined criteria

B: Restriction

C: Assumption

D: Constraint

Question #196
Your company provides IT support services for firmware upgrades. Your country's government has passed regulations stating that firmware of all telecommunication equipment must be upgraded to support IPv6. A government agency has approached your company to upgrade the firmware of all installed equipment at the major airports in the country.

For your company, this project is a result of which of the following:

A: Market demand

B: Strategic opportunity

C: Customer request

D: Legal requirement

Question #197

Your customer ask for a small change in the project, which was not budgeted in the project. It is a small effort as compared to the total project and you need the goodwill for a multimillion dollar on the pipeline. You will

A: Refuse to do the work

B: Agree to do the work at no charge

C: Do the work and bill him later

D: Assess the cost and schedule impact and tell them you will decide later

Question #198

Your goal as a project manager is to manage stakeholders to the best of your ability. However, if there are conflicts among stakeholders, they should usually be resolved in favor of:

A: Business Partner/Project Sponsor

B: Team Members

C: Customer

D: All Stakeholders

Question #199
Your project is coming to an end, and you are in the process of listing the activities that must be performed to close out the project.

Which of the following should be performed during the closing processes?

A: Seek legal counsel from the company's attorney prior to closing the project

B: Request final inspection reports for all vendor supplied products

C: Issue a formal notice of project completion to sellers

D: Issue payment schedules and requests

Question #200
Your project is in the final test stage, the user acceptance test. It meets all the product specs and is under planned costs. In term of schedule, this project is ahead. Your customer meets you and requested that he will not accept the product unless you make several changes.

What you should do is:

A: Get the list of the changes and estimate all of them. If the total cost is still within the baseline, you just do it

B: Estimate the costs and send this to your customer requesting contract modification

C: Ask the customer to file a Change request

D: Sit with the customer to review the product specs and tell him/her that you have completed the project

Answers

Every effort has been made to make this book as accurate as possible. However, there may be typographical and or content errors. Therefore, this book should serve only as a general guide and not as the ultimate source of subject information.

#1	B: 'Cost estimating.'
#2	D: 'Executing processes.'
#3	D: 'Cost control.'
#4	B: 'Project verification.'
#5	A: 'Resource planning.'
#6	B: 'Project performance.'
#7	B: 'Solicitation process.'
#8	B: 'Project scope management.'
#9	B: 'Process.'
#10	D: 'The first project is more attractive by app. 3%.'
#11	B: 'An identified risk occurs.'
#12	A: 'A planned response that defines the steps to be taken if an identified risk event should occur.'
#13	B: 'Cost Plus Fixed Fee.'
#14	A: 'Staffing Management Plan.'
#15	A: 'When team members are accountable to both functional and project managers.'
#16	B: 'Solicitation.'
#17	A: 'A group of projects managed in a coordinated way to obtain benefits not available from managing them individually.'
#18	D: 'Any undertaking with a definable time frame, well-defined objectives, and consumes both human and non-human resources with certain constraints.'
#19	B: 'Low position in the organization hierarchy.'
#20	D: 'Ability to handle power struggles and organizational games.'
#21	D: 'Responsibility assignment matrix.'
#22	B: 'What are the resources are available, at what times and in what patterns.'
#23	C: 'Avoidance.'

#24	C: 'How the project scope will be managed and how scope changes will be integrated into the project.'
#25	D: 'The number needed to control the project effectively.'
#26	B: 'Deliverable oriented grouping of project elements that organizes and defines the total scope of the project.'
#27	D: 'Salary.'
#28	C: 'Pareto Diagrams.'
#29	B: '$1400.'
#30	C: 'Performing organization.'
#31	B: 'Project management plan updates.'
#32	A: 'it is another term for the Statement of Work (SOW).' The product description is generally broader that a statement of work.
#33	D: 'Directing.'
#34	B: 'Ensure that the technical specifications are appropriately defined.'
#35	D: 'Reward and Recognition Systems.'
#36	D: 'Alternatives Identification.'
#37	D: 'Main consideration of both buyer and seller should be to maximize monetary return.'
#38	D: 'Care is taken to ensure that changes to the product scope are reflected in the project scope.'
#39	D: 'All projects have one cost baseline.'
#40	D: 'To be effective, a Project Manager should control all communications.'
#41	B: 'Fixed price contracts transfer risk to the seller if the design is unstable.'
#42	B: 'Contractual agreements with unions or other employee groups.'
#43	D: 'Corrective action based on causes.'
#44	B: 'Lessons learned.'
#45	C: 'Planning.'
#46	B: 'Elapsed Time.'
#47	D: 'You should try to solve a problem as soon as it is identified.'
#48	A: 'Theory Y (McGregor Model).'
#49	A: 'Consistently producing key results expected by stakeholders.'

#50	A: 'Consistently producing key results expected by stakeholders.'
#51	B: 'Making sure the information is received in its entirety, understood correctly and acknowledged.' For a communication to be successful the receiver needs to acknowledge its receipt to the sender, the receiver does not have to agree with the information.
#52	D: 'Bob must speak with the customer and issue a change request.'
#53	D: 'All of the above.'
#54	D: 'a and c.'
#55	A: 'Project.'
#56	A: 'Impacts of weather.'
#57	A: 'Address.'
#58	C: 'Conduct Procurements.'
#59	B: 'Subdividing the major project deliverables into smaller, more manageable components.'
#60	D: 'Scope planning.'
#61	A: 'Tell the stakeholders the work cannot be added.' PMI expects the project manager to manage! The best thing to do first is try to resolve the problem with the stakeholders. Only is that fails should the problem be escalated to the sponsor. Whilst planning and evaluation are normal 'first steps' in assessing a change, this work was formally excluded from the project before the Charter was signed. Therefore it should not be added without the sponsor's prior approval.
#62	A: 'Customer Satisfaction.'
#63	D: 'Developing a new product or service.'
#64	C: 'Convergent thinking.'
#65	A: 'Lessons learned.'
#66	D: '0.56.'
#67	C: 'Straight Line Depreciation.'
#68	A: 'Issue a Budget Update.'
#69	B: 'CPM.'
#70	D: 'Not known at time of the contract sign-off.'
#71	D: 'Cost.'
#72	D: 'Project D with NPV of $ 100,000.'
#73	D: 'All the statement above are true.'

#74	B: 'Document the lower quality level, ask the contractor for explanation and try to find a solution.'
#75	D: 'The utility theory.'
#76	D: 'Reduction in project cost.'
#77	D: 'b and c.'
#78	C: 'Internal Rate of Return.'
#79	C: 'Anticipating delays, the project had to be crashed to decrease duration.'
#80	D: 'Document the change and go ahead with implementing the change because no approvals are required.'
#81	B: 'Talk to your finance managers about why you think that they may be violating the standard accounting standards.'
#82	B: 'Laissez Faire.'
#83	B: 'Do not allow for the new requirement, because it will be a change in scope, and the customer did not explicitly mention the requirement.'
#84	D: 'Determining which decision yields the greatest expected value.'
#85	D: 'Dominator.'
#86	D: 'All of the above.'
#87	A: 'Unknown unknowns.'
#88	B: 'Project performance.'
#89	D: 'Obtain formal acceptance of the project scope and deliverables.'
#90	D: 'All of the above.'
#91	A: 'Improvements in amount of overtime worked.'
#92	A: 'Build.'
#93	C: 'Describes the processes required to ensure that the project will satisfy the needs for which it was undertaken.'
#94	C: 'Risk event, risk probability and the amount at stake.'
#95	D: 'Uncertain occurrences.'
#96	C: 'Risk analysis.'
#97	A: 'Initiation.'
#98	D: 'All of the above.'
#99	D: 'All of the above.'
#100	D: 'Source Selection.'
#101	B: 'Detriment.'
#102	B: 'Identifying, analyzing and responding to.'
#103	D: 'A and B.'

#104	B: 'Residual Risks.'
#105	A: 'Lateral thinking.'
#106	B: 'Developing a written scope statement as the basis for future project decisions.'
#107	C: 'Staffing pool description.'
#108	C: 'Project description.'
#109	B: 'Ensure that the team members understand how the work is to be done.'
#110	B: 'Project Integration Management.'
#111	C: 'Developing the cost performance baseline.' Developing the cost performance baseline is part of the Determine Budget process.
#112	C: 'Scope definition, activity duration estimating, cost budgeting.'
#113	B: 'Archive your learning in the project folder and share with other Project Managers.'
#114	C: 'the revision is the result of an approved scope change.' Budget updates are changes to an approved cost baseline. These values are generally revised only in response to approved changes in project scope.
#115	A: 'Decision-making.'
#116	C: 'Product description.'
#117	C: 'statistical independence.'
#118	C: 'Work packages.'
#119	A: 'Align the goals of the buyer and seller.'
#120	B: 'Improve Team performance.'
#121	B: 'WBS.'
#122	B: 'Revisions.'
#123	B: 'Revisions.'
#124	A: 'Procurement planning.'
#125	C: 'Its primary use is to request bids or proposals for the work it defines.'
#126	B: 'This is not acceptable quality because gold plating was done which is not advisable.'
#127	A: 'The connections between activities and project team members.' The RAM chart is used to illustrate the connections between work packages or activities and project team members.
#128	B: 'Project objectives, constraints and assumptions.'

#129	B: 'Deliverables.'
#130	A: 'Written, verbal, and non-verbal.'
#131	C: 'Expert judgment.'
#132	B: 'Sum of all the integrated management control plans.'
#133	C: 'Make it easier to assign resources to activity.'
#134	D: 'managing a project in terms of its objectives through all lifecycle phases and processes.'
#135	A: 'Project scope.'
#136	A: 'Project A.'
#137	A: 'Smoothing.'
#138	B: 'Benefit/Cost analysis.'
#139	B: 'Quality Planning.'
#140	B: 'Risk Register.'
#141	D: 'All of the above.'
#142	B: 'Compromising.'
#143	D: 'A and C.'
#144	C: '$26K.'
#145	B: 'Individual development.'
#146	D: 'Providing financial resources for the project.' The role of a project manager is to manage the project. The role of a customer/user is to use the product of the project. The role of project team members is to perform work of the project. The role of a sponsor is to provide financial resources for the project. Hence choice D is correct while choices A, B, and C are incorrect.
#147	B: 'Strong matrix.' Strong matrix organizations provide the project manager with a similar high level of authority to a projectized organization and full time project administration staff.
#148	D: 'Risk identification should be performed on a regular basis throughout the project.'
#149	A: 'Collaborating.'
#150	A: 'Cost management plan.'
#151	D: 'Prepare an independent estimate to check the proposed price of the different sellers.'
#152	D: 'Language, distance, culture, and knowledge.'
#153	B: 'Communications management plan.'
#154	D: 'Firm-fixed-price contract.'
#155	B: 'Formal acceptance documentation.'

#156	D: 'Government has passed a mandate that your project should not affect the neighborhoods adversely.' Choices A and B are results of some calculation. Choice C is an assumption, based on which further things can be calculated/projected. Choice D is a limitation under which the project needs to be undertaken. Hence choice D is correct while choices A, B, and C are incorrect.
#157	A: 'A strong matrix organization.'
#158	D: 'All of the above.'
#159	B: 'Ability of the stakeholders to influence final characteristics of the projects product increases as the project continues.'
#160	B: 'Contingency planning.'
#161	D: 'Inflation.'
#162	A: 'Recruitment practices.'
#163	C: 'Organizational Process Assets.'
#164	D: 'Inadequately defined requirements.'
#165	D: 'Inadequately defined requirements.'
#166	D: 'Formal project report.'
#167	C: 'Standard Deviation.'
#168	D: 'The influence of standards and regulations for a project is always known.'
#169	D: 'All of the above.'
#170	B: 'The administrative closure procedure addresses the terms and conditions of the contract for contract closure.'
#171	A: 'Procurement audits review the procurement process from plan purchases and acquisition to contract execution.'
#172	D: 'They limit the project team's options.'
#173	C: 'Schedule simulation.'
#174	A: 'Closeout.'
#175	C: 'If required, the Project Manager may try to use politics through power struggles or organizational games.'
#176	B: 'Unlike Facilitating processes, core processes have clear dependencies and are performed in same order in most projects.'
#177	B: 'Perform Additional Risk Response Planning to control the risk.'
#178	A: 'Objective Evaluation Criteria.'
#179	B: 'A deliverable oriented grouping of project components.'

#180	C: 'After the employee gets the promotion and is told of the transfer, you ask him to prepare a transition plan.'
#181	D: 'Perform updated risk identification and analysis.'
#182	B: 'Accept the gift because it is a custom in that country, and also inform your manager.'
#183	B: 'Constraint.'
#184	A: 'Integrated Change Control.'
#185	C: 'Corrective Action.'
#186	C: 'Providing support functions to Project Managers in the form of training, software, templates etc.'
#187	C: '13.' You began with 8 stakeholders (8*7)/2 = 28. You ended with 6 stakeholders (6*5)/2 = 15. You reduced communications channels by 28-15 = 13.
#188	D: '12 to 24 days.' To calculate the range at Sigma 3, add the Standard Deviation 3 times to the mean. Then subtract the Standard Deviation 3 times from the mean. 18 + 2 + 2 + 2 = 24. 18- 2 - 2- 2 = 12
#189	D: '9.' Variance is calculated by squaring the Standard Deviation. This is 3 x 3 = 9.
#190	A: 'The project has been cancelled while it was executed. At that time the project was behind schedule and on budget.'
#191	D: '4000.' Funds distribution is linear means you spend the same amount each period. In this case, divide the BAC/5 months = $4,000 per month. At the end of the first month, we should have spent $4,000.
#192	B: 'Delphi Technique.'
#193	B: 'Perform Administrative Closure.'
#194	B: '9000.' For Sum of the Years calculate the numerator based on a countdown of the years. This is 4, 3, 2, and 1 for a four year asset. In Year 2, the number we use is 3. The denominator is the sum of the years (1 + 2 + 3 +4 = 10). So, 3/10 x 30,000 = $9,000.
#195	D: 'Constraint.'
#196	C: 'Customer request.'
#197	D: 'Assess the cost and schedule impact and tell them you will decide later.'
#198	C: 'Customer.'
#199	C: 'Issue a formal notice of project completion to sellers.'
#200	C: 'Ask the customer to file a Change request.'

About the Author

FJ Russo works for one of the Big 5 Consulting Firms.

Throughout his 15-year project management career, he managed a large variety of projects: From $25K to multi-millions dollar projects, from two-week to multi-year consulting engagements, from business strategy to tactical road-mapping exercises, and from process engineering to software development activities.

From the Author

The 3-By-5 Steps: To Pass Your PMP® Certification

Practice and Pass the PMP® Exam, Volume 1

Practice and Pass the PMP® Exam, Volume 2

Practice and Pass the PMP® Exam, Volume 3

Practice and Pass the PMP® Exam, Volume 4

Practice and Pass the PMP® Exam, The 2000 Questions

www.ingramcontent.com/pod-product-compliance
Lightning Source LLC
Chambersburg PA
CBHW051903170526
45168CB00001B/217